A Churchill Treasury

A Churchill Treasury

SIR WINSTON'S PUBLIC SERVICE
THROUGH MEMORABILIA

BRIAN E. KRAPF

Pen & Sword
MILITARY

Published in Great Britain in 2023 by
PEN & SWORD MILITARY
An imprint of
Pen & Sword Books Ltd
Yorkshire - Philadelphia

© 2023 Brian Krapf

ISBN 978 1 39901 7 015

The right of Brian Krapf to be identified as Author of this work has been asserted by him in accordance with the Copyright, Designs and Patents Act 1988.

A CIP catalogue record for this book is available from the British Library

All rights reserved. No part of this book may be reproduced
or transmitted in any form or by any means, electronic or
mechanical including photocopying, recording or by any information storage
and retrieval system, without permission from the Publisher in writing.

Book Design by Dominic Allen

Printed and bound in India
by Replika Press Pvt. Ltd.

Pen & Sword Books Limited incorporates the imprints of Atlas, Archaeology, Aviation, Discovery, Family History, Fiction, History, Maritime, Military, Military Classics, Politics, Select, Transport, True Crime, Air World, Frontline Publishing, Leo Cooper, Remember When, Seaforth Publishing, The Praetorian Press, Wharncliffe Local History, Wharncliffe Transport, Wharncliffe True Crime and White Owl.

For a complete list of Pen & Sword titles please contact:
PEN & SWORD BOOKS LIMITED
47 Church Street, Barnsley, South Yorkshire, S70 2AS, England
E-mail: enquiries@pen-and-sword.co.uk
Website: www.pen-and-sword.co.uk
Or
PEN AND SWORD BOOKS
1950 Lawrence Rd, Havertown, PA 19083, USA
E-mail: Uspen-and-sword@casematepublishers.com
Website: www.penandswordbooks.com

Contents

	Dedication	7
	Forward by Randolph Churchill	9
	Introduction by Brian E. Krapf	11
1.	Lord Randolph	15
2.	Early Career	27
3.	First Lord of the Admiralty – Colonial Secretary – MP for Epping 1911-1924	49
4.	Chancellor of the Exchequer – Return to Admiralty 1924-1939	69
5.	World War II – The First Premiership	85
	Prime Minister Churchill	91
	Churchill and Roosevelt	137
	The "Big Three"	148
	The Battle of Britain	154
	Lend Lease	156
	Churchill's 1941 Christmas in Washington	164
	Wartime Conferences	167
	Mrs. Churchill's Aid to Russia Fund	183
	Victory Themed Pieces	184
6.	1945 Election – 1952 Second Premiership – Death in 1965	193

Dedication

TO STACY AND MAX
WITH LOVE

Portrait by Cecil Beaton

"WE WILL FINISH THE JOB"
"We shall not fail or falter; we shall not weaken or tire. Neither the sudden shock of battle, nor the long-drawn trials of vigilance and exertion will wear us down.
GIVE US THE TOOLS AND WE WILL FINISH THE JOB."
Mr. Churchill's reply to Mr. Roosevelt.

Celebrated British author A.P. Herbert served in the House of Commons as an independent MP for Oxford University from 1935-1950. During the Second World War, Herbert was the only non-commissioned officer in the House of Commons. He turned down a seat in Churchill's war cabinet, telling the Prime Minister, "No, thank you, sir. I'm quite happy where I am." Published here for the first time is Herbert's poem, *Vinnie Vil Vin*. Imagine the surprise of discovering this original poem when buying the postcard at an antiques fair stall.

Three dots and a dash (MORSE CO
Three dots and a long
The sign of the V, the hope of the free.
The victory flash, the liberty song.
Up with your thumbs, Victory comes.
Never say die — "Victory's nigh".
Tap on your plate, knock at the door
Bang on the gate, hammer the floor
Clap at the play, chalk on the tree
Hum in the hay "V for the free"
Say it with bells, say it with drums
Sing in your cells — "Victory comes"
Wherever the Hun thinks he has won
There shall he see the terrible "V"
Wherever the brute sits on his loot
There shall he hear a "V" in his ear
Victory! V!   Hitler may grin,
Viddle-de-dee!
VINNIE VILL VIN.
A·P· HERBERT.
M·P·

Foreword

My great-grandfather, Sir Winston Churchill, was a collector of historical memorabilia. On his desk at Chartwell sits his small ceramic bust of Admiral Lord Horatio Nelson, and his (much larger) Sèvres bust of Napoleon as First Consul by the sculptor Chaudet. Thanks to his remarkable achievements and towering fame, he would become—even during his lifetime—something of a collectible himself.

Brian Krapf has been a dedicated collector of Churchilliana for over three decades and is the Collections Columnist for the International Churchill Society. For the past seven years, he has treated the readers of the Churchill Bulletin to a monthly selection from his personal collection. He has shown us that these wonderful pieces of porcelain, textiles, paper, and other materials are illuminating historical artifacts. Now, Mr. Krapf has taken his passion a step further and published *A Churchill Treasury*, using these objects to tell the story of Sir Winston's decades of service to Britain and the world.

This book is quite splendid; each chapter is focused on a period of Sir Winston's public service and is richly illustrated with many never-before-seen items. I particularly appreciate the chapter featuring memorabilia of my great-great-grandparents, Lord and Lady Randolph Churchill. Sir Winston often cited Lord Randolph as the inspiration for his own career. Lady Randolph was a strongly independent American, renowned for her beauty and graciousness. Her many connections, both in America and Britain, helped Winston establish himself as a soldier and politician, as well as the world's highest-paid war correspondent.

Churchill's parting remarks to his Ministers upon his retirement as prime minister in 1955 included the enigmatic declaration, "Man is spirit." The transcendent nature of man's existence is illustrated in Brian's tremendous collection, each item of which carries the spirit of the great leader who inspired it.

A Churchill Treasury is a unique and fascinating prism through which to study my great-grandfather's life and career. Thank you, Brian, for your contributions to ICS, and for opening your archive of Churchilliana to share it with us all. Anyone with an interest in Sir Winston Churchill will enjoy this well-written and beautifully illustrated book.

Foreword by Randolph Churchill

Crockham Grange
Kent

December 2023

Introduction

Writing *A Churchill Treasury* has been both a pleasure and an honor. It is the first book to use period memorabilia as the basis for illustrating Sir Winston's career of public service.

All the pieces shown here are from my own collection. I've collected period *Churchilliana* for over three decades. Other collectors say I've assembled the finest collection in the United States. I don't know whether that's accurate, but I can say I approach my collecting with a tremendous passion. I am constantly on the hunt for something new and different. The search for *Churchilliana* finds me with boots on the ground at British antiques fairs, malls and shops, as well as both British and American online auctions. After all this time I see a lot of the same pieces, but there are still occasions when my continual searches unearth something previously unknown. The excitement of discovering something new and unique is the same as when I started searching for *Churchilliana* over 30 years ago. It's never tiring or boring.

Churchilliana is the term applied to Churchill collectibles. It encompasses a magnificent variety of paper, glassware, textiles, porcelain, badges, pottery, wood and metal. While there are differences in when, how, why and where these items were made, they all come together with the common focus and goal of telling the story of one of the world's greatest statesmen. Choosing which items to present was a process of deselection, rather than selection. I started with an outline of a particular area of Sir Winston's public service and eliminated what I thought were the more common pieces. The next step was to deselect pieces that were historic but had less visual appeal. What you see are pieces that are seldom seen, historic and visually appealing. There are several pieces that are being seen by the public for the first time.

Believe me when I say deselection was, in most respects, a tough process. Subjectively, I think every piece is important and historic. I'd show each and every one if space allowed.

I hope that *A Churchill Treasury* inspires readers to expand their awareness and appreciation of Sir Winston Churchill and motivates them to read, see and learn even more about him. Most will know he was Prime Minister of Great Britain during World War 2. However, many will discover that his 90 years on this earth were filled with a continual energy, drive and focus few possess. Aside from holding numerous government offices, he was an author, painter, soldier, pilot, brick mason, civil engineer, traveler, husband, father and grandfather. He raised a variety of animals and particularly doted on his dogs and cats. Sir Winston's greatest attribute, which set him apart and made him a true statesman, was his heartfelt compassion for his country and its people. No one loved Britain more. He would become emotional when touring bomb-stricken areas during the Blitz and meeting the people displaced from their homes and neighborhoods. His speeches were filled with genuine conviction and sincerity and were sources of inspiration and motivation when freedom was threatened. He never sugarcoated his words and maintained tremendous credibility amongst the British people. Today, we find his leadership a source of inspiration and often quote from his legendary speeches.

A book is far from a solo project and there are so many I need to thank for assistance, advice and support. First, thank you to the great photographer of the items pictured in *A Churchill Treasury*, my dear friend, Peter Nichols. Many Sundays were spent staging and photographing these historical pieces. Also, thank you to my Pen & Sword team, marketing editor, Tara Moran and production editor, Harriet Fielding. Both have been wonderful to work with over the past few years. Thank you, too, to Randolph Churchill for contributing the Forward, and to Paul Reid for his cover endorsement. Also, I'd be remiss if I did not thank my following friends and fellow Churchillians for their inspiration and motivation: Robert & Susan Fratkin, Daniel Moss, Simon Neil, Mark Sullivan, Rex Stark, Lee Pollack, David Freeman and Phil

Reed, MBE. Lastly, thank you to my wonderful family for your continued support and love.

I want to thank you, the readers of *A Churchill Treasury*, for wanting to learn more about Sir Winston Churchill. If you're so inclined, I wholeheartedly recommend that you join the International Churchill Society, www.WinstonChurchill.org. Through being a member, you will receive a monthly newsletter, a quarterly journal, and invitations to special Churchill-related events. More importantly, you will be linked to thousands of others around the world who study and admire Sir Winston, and work to preserve his memory for future generations.

With my best regards,

Brian E. Krapf
6 September 2023

CHAPTER ONE

Lord Randolph Churchill

The discussion of Churchill memorabilia begins with Lord Randolph Churchill, Sir Winston's father. While Sir Winston was descended from many generations of distinguished servants of their country, he often referred to his father as a primary source of inspiration for his own career of public service. Randolph Henry Spencer-Churchill was born 13 February 1849, the third son of John Spencer-Churchill, the Marquess of Blandford and his wife, the Marchioness of Blandford. Upon the death of John's father in 1857, they became the seventh Duke and Duchess of Marlborough. As the younger son of a Marquess, Randolph maintained the courtesy title of Lord.

The general election of February, 1874 proved to be a Conservative sweep, and Lord Randolph was elected to Parliament as the Conservative member for Woodstock, near the family seat of Blenheim Palace. A month later, on 15 April 1874, Lord Randolph married Jennie Jerome, the daughter of a prominent American businessman. The couple had two sons; Winston was born 30 November 1874, while Jack was born 4 February 1880.

In 1876, Lord Randolph moved to Ireland because of his feud with the Prince of Wales (later King Edward VII) and his threat to expose letters evidencing the Prince's role in a scandalous sexual affair. Lord Randolph returned to England in 1880 to stand for a seat in the House of Commons. He won and was a back bencher but gained notoriety by criticizing and obstructing Prime Minister William Gladstone and the Liberal majority. Although he was still not socially accepted due to his royal feud, Lord

Randolph worked his way up the political ladder. When the Conservative party returned to power in July, 1886, Lord Randolph was recognized as head of the House of Commons leadership. Prime Minister Lord Salisbury appointed Lord Randolph Churchill to the highly coveted position of Chancellor of the Exchequer.

Unfortunately, Lord Randolph's tenure did not last very long. From the time he was appointed Chancellor, he alienated many of his colleagues and defeated himself with his first budget. Lord Salisbury accepted his resignation on 20 December 1886. Lord Randolph published his resignation in the London Times three days later; many speculated that he expected a public outcry of support, but he failed to obtain one. After his resignation, he never again was placed in a position of leadership. He lost interest in politics and devoted a great deal of his time to horse racing.

Lord Randolph remained a member of the House of Commons until his death on 24 January 1895 at the young age of 45. In 1906, Winston Churchill published *Lord Randolph Churchill*, the definitive two volume biography of his father. In Sir Winston's 1930 autobiography, *My Early Life*, he laments Lord Randolph's death, writing, "he had hoped to one day join his father in Parliament." Many years later, in 1947, Sir Winston wrote his essay, *The Dream*, in which the long-passed Lord Randolph appears before his son for a meaningful conversation. However, this essay was not published until 30 January 1966, the first anniversary of his funeral. Whether by coincidence or fate, Sir Winston passed away 24 January 1965, 70 years to the day of Lord Randolph's death.

Items were produced to coincide with Lord Randolph's public service. As a Churchill collector, it is always fortuitous to find an item that documents Lord Randolph's place in history. Most date to around 1886 when Lord Randolph was at the peak of his popularity as Chancellor of the Exchequer. Since Lord Randolph only held this office for four months, most items associated with him from this time period are very rare and desirable.

These display plates were made in 1886 to celebrate Lord Randolph's appointment as Chancellor of the Exchequer. In the Victorian era, display plates and other porcelain pieces were popular household items and commemorated events, places or celebrity personalities. They survive today as historical collectibles.

WOODSTOCK ELECTION.

1880.   1880.

LORD RANDOLPH S. CHURCHILL

presents his compliments to

Mr Samuel Eccles

and thanks him sincerely for the very energetic support given him on Thursday 1st April, 1880.

BLENHEIM PALACE, 2nd APRIL, 1880.

This certificate was presented by Lord Randolph Churchill the day after the 1880 election. The oval image of Lord Randolph is an actual photograph, sized and glued on. Issued from Blenheim Palace, these certificates were presented to political supporters who played a significant role in Lord Randolph's election victory.

This bud vase by W.H. Goss includes the crest of the Churchill family above Lord Randolph's name. It was made at the time he was Chancellor of the Exchequer and reminded the public of his noble lineage.

This Christmas card dates to the 1880's and features the popular Lord Randolph. His head is attached with a paper insert, so that he gives a nod when the card is rocked.

When it was new, this large counter top tin contained either tea or ginger. The exterior is decorated with wonderful lithographed political scenes which relate to Prime Minister William Ewart Gladstone's Irish Home Rule Bill of 1886. The bill was defeated on 8 June 1886, but not until after vociferous debate in the House of Commons. On the tin, we see MPs who either supported or opposed the bill, including Lord Randolph, waving as they pass each other on a roller coaster. Likewise, we see another lithographed vignette of Lady Jennie Jerome Churchill, the wife of Lord Randolph and the mother of Sir Winston. Other scenes on the tin include a vignette of Prime Minister Gladstone and other notables related to the support or defeat of the Irish Home Rule bill.

Victorian glamour and fashion are evident in this large original period photograph of Lady Jennie Jerome Churchill, wife of Lord Randolph and mother of Sir Winston. Lady Churchill was a popular society figure and admired for her beauty but she also sponsored many charities and published a magazine. Circa 1880s, in period frame as discovered.

An enterprising tobacco manufacturer capitalized on Lord Randolph's popularity and named its cigarettes for Lady Churchill.

The three politicians featured on this dish- Liberal Prime Minister William Ewart Gladstone, Conservative leader Lord Randolph Churchill and Liberal leader Joseph Chamberlain- were central and pivotal to the Irish Home Rule bill of 1886. Gladstone introduced the bill while Churchill and Chamberlain (leading a faction of Liberal party MPs), opposed it. After the bill's defeat, Chamberlain formed the Liberal Unionist party which would join in coalitions with the Conservatives until the two parties formally merged in 1912. He was also the father of future prime minister Neville Chamberlain. One of these dishes sits on the table next to Sir Winston's reading chair in his study at his home, Chartwell.

During the Victorian era, parianware busts of prominent public figures were popular items for home display.

Lord Randolph Churchill

These woven silk portraits of Lord Randolph were manufactured in the 1880s by W.H. Grant of Coventry. They were part of a series of prominent politicians, which included Prime Ministers Gladstone and Disraeli as well as Joseph Chamberlain. The company also produced woven silk street scenes of old London, royalty, race horses and other popular themes.

Trade cards were a popular form of Victorian advertising. To catch the public's eye, many advertised businesses while also featuring riddles, puzzles or celebrities of the day. Given his popularity as a Conservative Party leader, Lord Randolph was among the numerous notables whose images were used as advertising. Saving these cards was a

In the above Silhouette Churchill does not appear so tall as Salisbury, nor Salisbury so tall as Gladstone, but if measured they will all be found of equal height.

N.B.—No other equality is to be inferred.

popular pastime and thankfully many have survived to be today's collectables. And... if you are looking for Lord Randolph in the puzzle card featuring Queen Victoria, turn the card onto its left side and look in Her Majesty's hair!

POST CARD

Dear Reader,

A so far unpublished story written by Sir Winston Churchill entitled "The Dream" has been acquired by the Sunday Telegraph & will appear <u>exclusively</u> this Sunday (January 30) Why not ask your Newsagent to deliver you a copy?

L.H. Dopson,
Oak Lodge,
Broad Lane,
Newdigate.

INNISMORE
Kingston
Taunton
Somerset

Sir Winston wrote his essay, *The Dream*, in 1947. In it, the spirit of Lord Randolph appears to him for a meaningful conversation. Sir Winston initially titled the essay *Private Article*, and showed it only to his family. Despite their belief it should be published, he refused. Sir Winston bequeathed the essay in his will to his wife, Clementine, who later donated it to Churchill College, Cambridge. On 30 January 1966, the first anniversary of Sir Winston's funeral, *The Dream* was published in the *Sunday Telegraph*. This advertising postcard was mailed to potential subscribers announcing that the essay would be published as encouragement to buy a copy.

CHAPTER TWO

Early Career

This chapter focuses on Sir Winston's Boer War experiences in 1899 through his tenure as Home Secretary in the Asquith government through 1911. It is important to note that Sir Winston was already in the public eye prior to this time, as he had served in the military and also stood for election for MP for Oldham and lost. Little if any material is available to document this earliest part of his public life. Therefore, we begin with the earliest material which can realistically be found in the marketplace; while items from this era can be found, they are still quite scarce.

This chapter begins in the year 1899 with the classic and well-told story of Churchill's capture by the Boers and subsequent escape. On 14 October, Churchill sailed to South Africa as a war correspondent for the *Morning Post*. On 15 November, he was captured and taken prisoner by the Boers during an armored train ambush near Chievely, South Africa. On 13 December, he escaped from the Boer prison in Pretoria and made his way back to England.

The year 1900 is highlighted by two major events. On 1 October, Churchill was elected the Conservative MP for Oldham. Two months later, on 1 December, he began his North American lecture tour, enthralling audiences in the United States and Canada with recounts of his experiences in South Africa.

On 31 May 1904, Churchill left the Conservative Party, "crossed the floor," and joined the Liberal Party. In 1905, Prime Minister AJ Balfour resigned and Sir Henry Campbell-Bannerman formed a government pending a January election. On 13 December, Churchill was named Undersecretary of State for the Colonies in the Campbell-Bannerman government. This appointment allowed him to speak about colonial affairs before the House of Commons, as his chief, Lord Elgin served in the House of Lords.

As the year 1906 began, two significant events occurred in Churchill's life. First, on 2 January, he published the biography of his late father, *Lord Randolph Churchill*. Next, on 13 January, he was elected MP for Manchester North-West in a Liberal Party election sweep.

On 5 April 1908, Prime Minister Campbell-Bannerman resigned due to ill health. H.H. Asquith became Britain's new prime minister. On 12 April, Churchill joined the Asquith cabinet as President of the Board of Trade. Only 34 years old, this was his first cabinet appointment and he was one of the youngest cabinet officers in British history. This position was first established in the 17th century and still exists today. The President of the Board of Trade oversees a committee which promotes and regulates trade and commercial activity.

On 24 April, Churchill was defeated in Manchester North-West in a by-election. He had to hastily find another seat, as holding office was a requirement for serving in a cabinet post. On 9 May, he was elected MP for Dundee, thus also remaining in the Asquith government. Lastly, 1908 was a significant year in Churchill's personal life. On 11 August, he became engaged to his future wife, Miss Clementine Hozier. The couple was married on 1 September.

On 29 April 1909, the Chancellor of the Exchequer, David Lloyd George, along with the President of the Board of Trade, Winston Churchill, introduced the People's Budget. This was a revolutionary concept promoted by the Liberal Party that redistributed wealth through unprecedented taxes on land and income to fund new social welfare programs. These included old age pensions and improved working conditions and benefits, particularly for miners. The People's Budget passed in the House of Commons but was rejected by the House of Lords, which was dominated by Conservatives. The government considered the failure of the budget's passage a constitutional crisis and called for a general election which was held 15 January-10 February 1910. Liberals narrowly won with a two-seat majority, later increased in a coalition with members of the Irish Parliamentary Party. Asquith again formed a government. Churchill was reelected as MP for Dundee and remained in the Asquith government as President of the Board of Trade. After the election, he proposed the abolition of the House of Lords in a cabinet memorandum, suggesting that it be replaced by either a unicameral system or a new, smaller second chamber that lacked a natural advantage for the Conservatives. In April, the Lords relented and the People's Budget passed into law. Another general election was held 3-19 December 1910. The Government called this second election in one year to obtain a mandate for the Parliament Act of 1911, which would reduce and restrict the House of Lords' ability to block economic legislation. Churchill continued to campaign against the House of Lords and was a vocal proponent of the Parliament Act of 1911. When all was done, the Act was passed, Asquith remained Prime Minister as a result of the Liberal-Irish Parliamentary Party coalition, and Churchill continued as President of the Board of Trade.

On 14 February, Churchill was named Home Secretary in the Asquith government. This was again a cabinet position, and has been described as the secretary of state for domestic affairs. As Home Secretary, Churchill oversaw law enforcement in England and Wales, matters of national security, immigration issues and Britain's prison and probation system.

In November 1910, miners were striking across South Wales and clashes between the police and protesters escalated. In Tonypandy, rioting took place over the weekend of 9 November. Miners wrecked shops in the town centre and attacked property belonging to pit owners. At the time, constabularies in South Wales were small; Churchill, as Home Secretary, sent a detachment of Metropolitan Police to help support the local police. When it was evident the police were not enough of a force to quash the violence, Churchill then deployed a unit of the 18th Hussars. He was reportedly reluctant to do so but was requested to by the local chief of police. Residents resented the presence of military troops, who stayed in the area to help maintain peace. Two protesters were killed but its unclear how they died. Churchill's reputation in Wales suffered as a result of sending in troops.

On 3 January 1911, Churchill, as Home Secretary, accompanied police to observe their containment of London anarchists in the "Battle of Sidney Street." This action was the culmination of a series of events that began in December 1910, when three policemen were killed and two others wounded in the attempted burglary of a London jewelry store by a gang of Latvian immigrants. The police were informed that the two remaining gang members who had not been killed or captured were hiding at 100 Sidney Street in Stepney. The police evacuated local residents and on 3 January, a gun battle subsequently ensued. Having weapons inferior to those used by the anarchists, the police sought assistance from the army. This marked the first time the police had requested the army's intervention to quash an armed standoff. At the time, the Metropolitan Police and the City of London Police both patrolled and serviced London and came under the control of the Home Secretary. Officers in charge at the scene called the Home Office and obtained permission from Churchill to bring in a detachment of Scots Guards stationed at the Tower of London. The siege lasted about six hours. A building caught fire and the London Fire Brigade found two bodies while extinguishing the blaze. Later the building collapsed, killing a fireman.

The "Battle of Sidney Street" was the first siege in Britain to be filmed. Footage taken by *Pathé News* included images of Home Secretary Winston Churchill accompanying the police. His presence at the scene and level of involvement were both criticized. Churchill had arrived to observe the action but his role in the siege remains unclear. Biographers contend he played no operational role, but a Metropolitan Police report notes he made command decisions. In a letter to the *London Times*, Churchill publicly denied any command responsibility, leaving all such decisions to the police.

With this brief overview of Winston Churchill's early career, please enjoy the illustrations and explanations of the artifacts of this time period in the pages that follow.

"His description of his escape is an Epic poem."—LORD WOLSELEY.

WINSTON SPENCER Churchill.

Warrior, Writer and M.P., in his Famous Lecture

The War as I Saw It.

| With the Account of His Capture and Escape. |

MASSEY MUSIC HALL | SATURDAY, DEC. 29
Reserved seats, $1.50, $1, 75c. Admission, 50c.

The Mendelssohn Choir of Toronto.

A. S. VOGT, Conductor

CONCERT. Massey Ha[ll]
Thursday, January 24th, 1901. Ch[oral] voices. Artists assisting: FANNY . FIELD-ZEISLER, pianiste; Gertrude M[...] contralto. Subscribers' list at Nordheime[r] $1; $1.50 section entirely subscribed for.

On 1 December 1900, two months after being elected the Conservative MP for Oldham, Churchill began his North American lecture tour, enthralling audiences in the United States and Canada with recounts of his South African experiences. These two Toronto newspaper advertisements were typically how Churchill's lectures were advertised.

DECEMBER 31. 1900.

AMUSEMENTS.

Massey Hall. | To-night 8.15.

Winston Spencer Churchill.

"The War as I Saw It."
CHAIRMAN—COL OTTER. O.D.C.
Reserved Seats $1.50, $1.00, 75c. Rush seats, 500 at 50c.

GRAND | House Opera | Matinee To-day.
LAST PERFORMANCE TO-NIGHT OF
THE GREAT KELLAR
Next Week—ARIZONA.

Shea's THEATRE
Week f D ec. 31

Arrivée à Pretoria des prisonniers du train blindé d'Estcourt (Lord Churchill à gauche en casquette).

La Guerre Anglo-Boer

This very interesting postcard was printed in Brussels shortly after the end of the Boer War as part of the publisher's Transvaal Series. At the time it was published, Churchill would have already embarked on his post-war North American lecture tour. The card presents a sepia tinted image of the Boer prison train which transported Churchill after his capture, along with other prisoners at Pretoria from Estcourt. The card's caption specifically notes "Lord Churchill" is the person wearing a cap, with his back to the camera.

This stereoscope card presents one of the earliest public images of Winston Churchill, as a war correspondent during the Boer War. It was produced in 1900 by the Keystone View Company as part of their Boer War images series. By the time this stereoscope card was published, Churchill had already attained notoriety for his famous escape from Boer imprisonment in Pretoria. Rather than returning home indefinitely, he joined General Redvers Buller's army on its march to relieve British troops at the Siege of Ladysmith and to retake Pretoria. Although he continued as a war correspondent for *The Morning Post* with a salary of £250 per month, he also obtained a commission in the South African Light Horse. Churchill later recounted this period of his life in articles for *The Strand* magazine, in his autobiography, *My Early Life*, and in his later book, *Ian Hamilton's March*.

11819—Winston Spencer Churchill, the Famous War Correspondent, Bloemfontein, South Africa.

This portrait of 26 year old Winston Churchill was published on 27 September 1900 in *Vanity Fair* magazine, the week he was elected the Conservative MP for Oldham. It was created by Sir Leslie Matthew Ward, a noted British portrait artist and caricaturist whose work was regularly published by *Vanity Fair* under the pseudonyms "Spy" and "Drawl." The portraits were published as chromolithographs in the magazine while also reproduced on better paper and sold as prints.

In the early 1900's, Churchill was pictured in postcard series, tobacco cards and magic lantern slides because he already held important government positions by his early 30s.

On 13 December 1905, Churchill was named Undersecretary of State for the Colonies in the Campbell-Bannerman government. This appointment allowed him to speak about colonial affairs before the House of Commons, as his chief, Lord Elgin served in the House of Lords. This postcard includes Churchill as one of King Edward VII's "Empire Builders."

The month-long Colonial Conference was held in London beginning 15 April 1907 and was chaired by Prime Minister Henry Campbell-Bannerman. At the conference, self-governing British colonies were given dominion status. The possibilities of Irish Home Rule and Indian self-governance were also discussed. Churchill was amongst the participants as Undersecretary for the Colonies as shown on this souvenir postcard.

This original pen and ink sketch of Winston Churchill and other participants at the Colonial Conference was created by noted editorial artist Ralph Cleaver for the *Illustrated London News*. Cleaver signed the sketch in the bottom left hand corner and various handwritten pre-publication draft comments are found along the bottom margin. An archive of Cleaver's editorial illustrations can be found at the Victoria & Albert Museum in London.

On 13 January 1906, Churchill was elected MP for Manchester North-West in a Liberal Party election sweep. He held this seat until defeated in a by-election on 24 April 1908. Pictured here is a campaign card, promoting Churchill's re-election as a free trade proponent. Also pictured here are two exceptionally rare glass slides giving us a glimpse of how Manchester looked during the 1908 by-election.

FREE TRADE FOR EVER AND CHURCHILL NOW!

With his 1908 election defeat in Manchester, Churchill faced a predicament. He was still in the Asquith cabinet as President of the Board of Trade. However, he had to hastily find another MP position, as holding office was a requirement for serving in a cabinet post. On 9 May 1908, he was elected MP for Dundee. This handwritten poem reflects the urgency in Churchill's needing "a seat." Churchill would serve as Liberal MP for Dundee until 1922.

38 – A Churchill Treasury

PEERS v. PEOPLE!

VOTE FOR THE BUDGET!

Which puts the Burden on the Broadest Shoulders.

LIBERALS AND WORKING MEN!
SUPPORT THE
YORKSHIRE EVENING NEWS

Insist upon having it and refuse Substitutes.

YOUR GREATEST NEED IS A STRONG PRESS!

The front of this card shows a composite of all members of the Asquith government, including Churchill as President of the Board of Trade. The back shows support for the People's Budget, which was championed by Churchill and David Lloyd George.

Early Career - 39

As President of the Board of Trade, Churchill was an invited speaker at this 1909 reception hosted by the City Liberal Club.

Reception.

MONDAY, JUNE 28th, 1909.

8.30 to 9.15. Reception of Guests by
THE COUNTESS BEAUCHAMP.

9.15. Song - "The Sailor's Grave" - - *Sullivan.*
MR. DAVID EVANS.

Song - "Je veux vivre" (*Romeo et Juliette*) *Gounod.*
MISS DOROTHY WEBB, A.R.C.M.

9.30. Speeches.
The Right Hon. EARL BEAUCHAMP, K.C.M.G.,
AND
The Right Hon. WINSTON S. CHURCHILL, M.P.
(*President of the Board of Trade*).

10.5. Song - "Glorious Devon" - *Edward German.*
MR. DAVID EVANS.

Song - "I hear you calling me" *Charles Marshall.*
MISS DOROTHY WEBB, A.R.C.M.

REFRESHMENTS served in the SMOKING ROOM.

From 8.30 to 11 o'clock ASHTON'S AUSTRO-HUNGARIAN BAND will play Selections.   (*For Programme see other side.*)

At age 33, Churchill was appointed to his first cabinet office, President of the Board of Trade, by Prime Minister H.H. Asquith. He held this office from 1908-1910. This postcard was published in March 1909 by Rotary Photographic, Ltd as part of a small series of important men of the day. It features a caricature of Churchill drawn by Harold Smith, a portraitist for *The Bystander*, a popular weekly tabloid later famous for publishing Bruce Bairnsfather's "Old Bill" series during the Great War.

PHILCO SERIES 3494E.
RT. HON. WINSTON SPENCER CHURCHILL.

MISS CLEMENTINE HOZIER

When he married Clementine Hozier on 1 September 1908, Winston Churchill was Liberal MP for Dundee and President of the Board of Trade in the Asquith government. The wedding of such a prominent public figure warranted the publishing of commercially sold postcards.

Early Career - 41

These two graphic postcards depict the issues of the 1910 elections. The first card is titled *Liberal Burstup* and depicts Liberal party leaders, including Churchill, being thrown from a biplane. Chancellor of the Exchequer David Lloyd George is trying desperately to hold onto the People's Budget. The second card depicts Lloyd George, Churchill and Prime Minister Asquith toppling the House of Lords by making a *peer dis-a-peer*.

The Conservatives still considered Churchill a turncoat for "crossing the floor" and joining the Liberal party. In 1910, they published this pamphlet depicting Churchill as a clown, hypocrite and spoiled son of privilege.

Early Career - 43

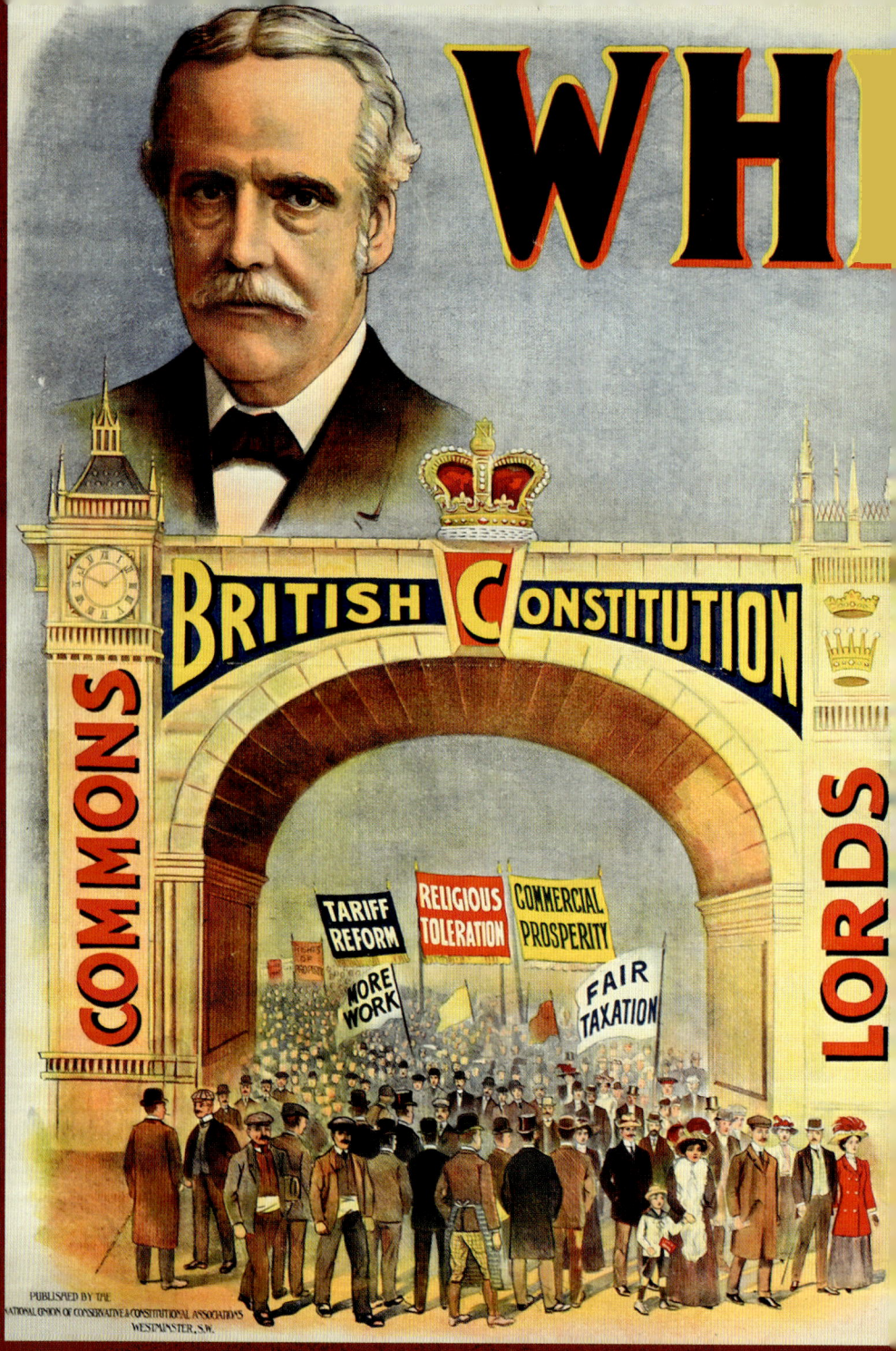

The issues to be decided by the December 1910 general election are elegantly depicted on this giant (5 ft x 3ft) poster published by the National Union of Conservative and Constitutional Associations. Voters could choose tradition and stability by re-electing former Prime Minister AJ Balfour and the Conservatives, or the smashing of traditional values by re-electing current Prime Minister Asquith and the Liberals. The vignette at the bottom depicts Lloyd George, Churchill

and Asquith firing the cannon which has destroyed the pillars of a stable British government. The 1910 general election resulted in a hung Parliament; the Conservatives received more votes but the Liberals, through their coalitions, added two more seats in the House of Commons. Prime Minister Asquith again formed a government in which Churchill continued serving as President of the Board of Trade.

There were two elections called in 1910 over the issues of passage of the People's budget and the abolition of the House of Lords in favor of one governing body. This porcelain figure was made by Carlton in 1910 and depicts John Citizen, hunched over as he tries to carry the burdens of unemployment, inadequate housing and unfair taxation. These were the issues sought to be remedied when the Liberal Party, led by David Lloyd George and Winston Churchill, sought passage of the People's Budget.

On 14 February 1911, Churchill was named Home Secretary in the Asquith government. This was again a cabinet position, and he oversaw law enforcement in England and Wales, matters of national security, immigration issues and Britain's prison and probation system. The 23 June 1911 coronation of King George V and Queen Mary occurred during Churchill's tenure. He issued this pass for the reviewing stand at the Admiralty Archway at Whitehall. Note that ladies were requested not to wear large hats.

indy little gasbag.
iterfering fool
o idea of anything
tubborn as a mule
onypandy tradesmen
we you quite a lot
ow's the time to make you

atch it pretty hot
elping silly suffragettes
nder durance vile
endering the law an "ass"
adging votes the while
ow the Policemen love you
liot ! give it up,
ttle lying nincompoop
oathsome Blenheim Pup.

o be Sung to the tune of " Gaily Sings the Donkey as he goes to grass."

In November, 1910, miners were striking across South Wales and clashes between the police and protesters escalated. In Tonypandy, rioting took place over the weekend of 9 November. Churchill, as Home Secretary, sent police reinforcements and later an army detachment to help the overwhelmed local constabulary quash the riots and restore order. Churchill's reputation in Wales suffered as a result of sending in troops. This palm card makes use of Churchill's name to criticize him and portray him as inept. It was published around the time of the Tonypandy riots.

On 3 January 1911, Churchill, as Home Secretary, accompanied police to observe their containment of London anarchists in what became known as the "Battle of Sidney Street." This was the first siege in Britain to be filmed and footage taken by *Pathé News* included images of Churchill. His presence at the scene and level of involvement were both criticized. A series of postcards was produced to memorialize the event. These two show Churchill as he accompanied the police.

"THE BATTLE OF STEPNEY": Mr Winston Churchill surrounded by Detectives and Armed Police

Mr Winston Churchill (Home Secretary).

CHAPTER THREE

First Lord of the Admiralty – Colonial Secretary – MP for Epping 1911-1924

This chapter includes historical items for Churchill's 1911 appointment as First Lord of the Admiralty in the Asquith government, through his 1924 election as MP for Epping. This period of time, 1911 through 1924, only comprises thirteen years, but it includes the Great War and its aftermath, Churchill's tenure as Secretary of State for the Colonies and a series of election losses until he was elected MP for Epping. In terms of historical Churchill items, we see more commercially-produced material, since Britain and her leaders were pictured and promoted on items during the Great War. Churchill's image was used on commercially-made badges, porcelain, paper and textiles. Again, a brief timeline is provided to serve as an overview of this period of Churchill's public service.

On 25 October 1911, Churchill was appointed First Lord of the Admiralty in the Asquith government. In this position, he was the civilian head of the Royal Navy and oversaw all aspects of its management. He immediately set to work modernizing the navy. For the next two years, he converted the British fleet from coal to oil. He also commissioned the construction of new high-speed ships with 15-inch guns. Also, recognizing the increasing use of aircraft, Churchill established the Royal Navy Air Service

On 28 June 1914, Archduke Franz Ferdinand of Austria-Hungary was assassinated at Sarajevo. Realizing that war was likely, Churchill ordered the British fleet to its war station at Scapa Flow in the Orkney Islands on 1 August. Three days later, Britain declared war against Germany.

On 3 January 1915, supported by First Sea Lord Admiral Jackie Fisher and the Secretary of State for War, Lord Herbert Kitchener, Churchill proposed a naval and military attack on the Dardanelles. He believed that Royal Navy sea power would force open the straits. The plan was to relieve Turkish pressure on the Russians in the Caucasus by staging attacks against Turkey in the Dardanelles. Approval was given and, in March 1915, an Anglo-French task force attempted a naval bombardment of Turkish defenses in the Dardanelles. In April, the Mediterranean Expeditionary Force began its assault at Gallipoli. Both of these campaigns failed and Churchill was deemed responsible by many MPs, particularly Conservatives. On 15 May, Churchill resigned as First Lord of the Admiralty and Admiral Fisher resigned as First Sea Lord.

Shortly thereafter, Prime Minister Asquith formed a coalition government with the Conservative Party, which demanded that Churchill be given no war related cabinet positions. On 27 May, he was appointed Chancellor of the Duchy of Lancaster, a position which held status, but required very little work; one of its main duties was to appoint rural judges. Aside from his public service, another significant event occurred only a few months later; on 2 July, Churchill began his first oil painting, a pastime he would enjoy for the next fifty years.

On 11 November 1915, Churchill resigned from the Asquith government. Although still an MP, he joined the Army with the rank of major and was attached to the 2nd Grenadier Guards, with service on the Western Front. In January 1916, he was temporarily promoted to lieutenant-colonel and given command of the 6th Royal Scots Fusiliers. After a period of training, the battalion was moved to a sector of the Belgian Front near Ploegsteert (often called "Plug Street"). For over three months, they faced continual shelling although there was no German offensive. In May, the 6th Royal Scots Fusiliers were merged into the 15th Division. Churchill did not request a new command and instead sought permission to leave active service.

On 7 May 1916, Churchill, still MP for Dundee, returned from military service to London and Parliament. Back in the House of Commons, Churchill spoke out on war issues, calling for conscription to be extended to the Irish, greater recognition of soldiers' bravery, and for the introduction of steel helmets for troops. Even with the passage of time, he was still often blamed for the failure of the Gallipoli campaign by Conservatives and the pro-Conservative press. On 18 July 1916, Prime Minister Asquith announced the establishment of the Dardanelles Commission to investigate the causes of the campaign's failure. Churchill initially thought he would be able to attend meetings of the commission, but they were held in secret. Instead he testified before the commission in September and arranged for other witnesses whom he felt important to also offer testimony. The final report of the commission was issued in 1919. It outlined significant problems with the planning and execution of the campaign which were exacerbated by personality clashes and supply shortages. However, Churchill was exonerated; the commission placed no blame on him personally for the campaign's failure.

Seven months later, on 6 December 1916, David Lloyd George succeeded Herbert Asquith as Prime Minister. On 6 April 1917, the United States entered the Great War. On 18 July, Churchill was appointed Minister of Munitions in Lloyd George's coalition government. On 30 July, Churchill won the by-election at Dundee and was returned as MP.

On 1 April 1918, the Royal Flying Corps and the Royal Naval Air Service merged to become the Royal Air Force. In July 1918, in his capacity as Assistant Secretary of the US Navy, Franklin Roosevelt made a visit to Great Britain. He toured British and American bases and met with several members of the British war cabinet, including PM Lloyd George and Foreign Secretary AJ Balfour. Similarly, he was granted a forty-five-minute audience with King George V. On 29 July Roosevelt met Churchill for the first time at a dinner at Gray's Inn in London. He was thoroughly unimpressed and later recalled Churchill "acted like a stinker." Despite FDR's recollection, Churchill later did not remember their first meeting.

On 11 November, an armistice ended the fighting of the Great War. With the war over, Lloyd George called a general election for Saturday, 14 December 1918. During his re-election campaign for MP for Dundee,

Churchill supported the nationalization of the railways, a control on monopolies, tax reform, and the creation of a League of Nations. He was re-elected and Lloyd George remained Prime Minister although the Conservatives won a majority.

On 9 January 1919, Churchill was appointed Secretary of State for War and Secretary of State for Air in the Lloyd George government. He was responsible for demobilizing the postwar British Army, although he convinced Lloyd George to keep soldiers on active duty to serve in the British Army of the Rhine. Churchill was also opposed to punitive reparations for Germany. Lloyd George privately agreed but felt compelled to publicly take a different position with President Wilson and French Prime Minister Georges Clemenceau. 1919 also saw Churchill publicly supporting anti-Bolsheviks in the Russian civil war. Lastly, he began his Great War memoirs, *The World Crisis*.

On 14 February 1921, Churchill was appointed Secretary of State for the Colonies in the Lloyd George government. In March, he convened the Cairo Conference to settle borders within the Middle East. Colonel T.E. Lawrence, the famed Lawrence of Arabia, was his chief advisor.

March also witnessed the first public exhibition of Churchill's paintings; it took place in Paris, with Churchill exhibiting under a pseudonym.

On 1 April, Churchill resigned as Secretary of State for Air. On 6 December, he helped negotiate the Irish Treaty, signed by Lloyd George, Michael Collins and Arthur Griffith.

On 19 October 1922, Lloyd George resigned following the withdrawal of the Conservatives from his coalition government. There were many reasons for the dissolution of Lloyd George's coalition, but a significant one arose in September 1922, when Turkey threatened to occupy the Dardanelles neutral zone, which was policed by British forces based in Chanak. Churchill and Lloyd George favored military opposition to any Turkish advance but the Conservatives in the coalition government opposed it. As a result, the Conservatives withdrew from the coalition, prompting the call for the November 1922 general election.

Upon Lloyd George's government coalition being dissolved, Churchill resigned as Colonial Secretary. In November, he was left an unexpected inheritance by a distant relative; he used these funds to purchase Chartwell, near Westham, Kent, for £5,000. Over the next two years, he spent another £17,000 renovating and refurbishing the home. All the while, he continued writing The World Crisis, which netted him £20,000. On 15 November, Churchill was defeated as MP for Dundee by Prohibitionist Edwin Scrygmour, who had tried to take the seat for 14 years. For the first time in 22 years – since 1908 – Churchill had no seat in the House of Commons.

Churchill spent much of the next six months at the Villa Rêve d'Or near Cannes, focused on painting and continuing to write his autobiographical history of the Great War, The World Crisis. Volume I was published on 6 April 1923. Volume II was published in October. In all, five volumes in six parts were published between 1923 and 1931.

After the 1923 general election was called, seven Liberal associations asked Churchill to stand as their candidate. Still without a seat in the House of Commons, Churchill ran as a Liberal Free Trader for MP for West Leicester. He was defeated on 6 December in the by-election. Ramsay MacDonald's Labour government took power, defeating a Conservative-Liberal coalition. Given Churchill's prior anti-Bolshevik stance after the Great War, he strongly opposed the MacDonald government's decision to loan money to Soviet Russia.

On 19 March 1924, alienated by Liberal support for Labour, Churchill stood for election in the Westminster Abbey by-election as an independent anti-socialist candidate but was defeated. In May, while addressing a Conservative meeting in Liverpool, he declared there was no longer a place for the Liberal Party in British politics. He asserted that Liberals must back the Conservatives to stop Labour and to ensure the defeat of socialism. In the 29 October 1924 general election, Churchill won election for MP at Epping, calling himself a "Constitutionalist". He would hold this seat and the derivative seat for Woodford, through 1964.

RT. HON. WINSTON CHURCHILL.

As one who hitherto has won
Our confidence complete—
We Britons—in this crisis— trust
The "power behind the fleet."

These Great War era postcards depict Winston Churchill as First Lord of the Admiralty. Given his relatively short tenure after the war began, the Churchill cards are not as common as post cards depicting other wartime military personalities. In one below, King George V is flanked on the right by Prime Minister Herbert Asquith and First Lord of the Admiralty Churchill. Interestingly, the two figures

to the left of King George V are General John French, Commander-in-Chief of the British Expeditionary Force and General Ian Hamilton, Commander-in-Chief of the Home Army. In another, to the left, Churchill is pictured along with Foreign Secretary Edward Grey and Britain's timeless hero, Admiral Horatio Nelson.

These two porcelain busts of Churchill as First Lord of the Admiralty were made by two leading porcelain manufacturers, Shelley and Goss, in 1914-1915 as part of their series depicting wartime leaders. While production of both series continued further into the war, the Churchills were discontinued after his resignation from the Admiralty in 1915.

One of the perks of being First Lord of the Admiralty was having use of the Admiralty's yacht, HMS *Enchantress*. During the three peacetime years Churchill spent at the Admiralty, 1911-1914, he spent eight months aboard Enchantress. He visited hundreds of ships and naval establishments throughout the British Isles and the Mediterranean, but also enjoyed the use of the yacht for his pleasure. On many voyages, Churchill would be accompanied by his wife, friends and associates.

The photographs shown here were previously unknown and are being published for the first time. They were acquired directly from the family of an *Enchantress* crewman. We do not know when or where they were taken, but they are extremely unique, historical and offer a glimpse into the private life of one of the world's most public men. While other photographs of Churchill at leisure have been published, Churchill at the surf with his trousers rolled, Churchill playing golf and Churchill in yachting attire are distinguished from the images typically seen.

As First Lord of the Admiralty, Churchill is pictured with other British military leaders on this wartime tea tin.

This bisque figurine was created in 1915 to parody Churchill and reflects the public opinion against him in the critical aftermath of Gallipoli. Sir Joseph Porter is the bumbling and inept Lord of the Admiralty in Gilbert and Sullivan's *HMS Pinafore*. He is the child of privilege, having obtained his office not through military skill and experience, but through patronage. Images of Sir Joseph consistently depict him as a much older man; this figurine unmistakably depicts a much younger Winston Churchill. After Gallipoli, newspapers compared Churchill to Porter, painting him to appear as an inept, privileged office holder who made tactical naval decisions resulting in a disastrous outcome.

LONDON'S CALL TO ARMS.

MONSTER DEMONSTRATION
. at the .
London Opera House, Kingsway,
By kind permission of the Directors.

On Friday, September 11th, 1914, at 8 p.m.

SPEAKERS:
Right Hon. WINSTON CHURCHILL, M.P.
Right Hon. F. E. SMITH, K.C., M.P.
Mr. WILLIAM CROOKS, M.P.
THE MARQUESS OF LINCOLNSHIRE, K.G. . In the Chair.
Mr. J. F. REMNANT, M.P. . . . . In the Vice-Chair.

The Joint Committee of the National Liberal Club and the Constitutional Club request the company of

Miss Ethel Curtis

R.S.V.P. to
The Secretary,
National Liberal Club,
Whitehall Place, S.W.

Entrance in Sardinia Street.

I'm Thinking of YOU 2 Everyday.

At the Naval Camp, BLANDFORD, 1915.

I haven't got time to drop you a line,
  And I thought perhaps you might grieve;
So I send you this card just to say I'm alright,
  And long to see you again when "on leave."

When Old England's Call for more men to fight
  For her honour—in me caused a thrill;
I felt fight I must or else I should "bust,"
  So I'm in CAMP, near BLANDFORD until—

The work it is hard—for we're "at it" all day,
  And sometimes half of the night;
But we're hardening to it and getting quite fit,
  And thank goodness for "grub" we're alright.

My duty calls me, and we're shortly to go
  To the place where the fightin' is done;
And once the NAVAL BOYS get grip on the foe,
  There's no leaving go till they've won.

So cheer up, my dear, tho' parted we are,
  And though I'm so far away;
My loved ones are ever *first* in my thoughts,
  I'm thinking of YOU every day.
                                    Copyright.

POST CARD.

Mrs. S. Martin
48 Goldwell Rd
Fakenham
Norwich
Norfolk

Benton & Co., 60, North Road, Brighton.

Tuesday 16th

Dear Ma & Dad
Just a line to let you now im in thee pink we are parading before Mr Churchill to morrow 43 Dorset St. We are now Blandford Winsoled Dorset Churchills Army

please write to that address

First Lord of the Admiralty – Colonial Secretary – MP for Epping 1911-1924

In the era when fountain pens were used, blotters were popular advertising giveaways for merchants and businesses. As a well known public figure, Churchill was included on this merchant's blotter to help boost attention and sales.

This rare and personal real photo postcard is published here for the first time and shows the Churchills' home staff in 1912. Unfortunately, only one of the twelve staff is identified; from a penciled notation on the back, Miss Chick is second from the right in the front row. The Churchills had resided at 33 Eccleston Square in London since Churchill purchased the home in Spring, 1909. In May 1913, the Churchills moved to Admiralty House, the official residence of the First Lord of the Admiralty. 33 Eccleston Square was then rented for the next three years to Sir Edward Grey, the Foreign Secretary.

This set of clothing buttons is preserved on their original sales card and feature prominent Liberals of the Asquith government. These include Prime Minister H.H. Asquith, Chancellor of the Exchequer David Lloyd George, Secretary of State for War Viscount Richard Haldane, Foreign Secretary Sir Edward Grey, First Lord of the Admiralty Winston Churchill and President of the Board of Trade John Burns.

First Lord of the Admiralty Winston Churchill is posed like Britannia, ready to rule the waves in this Great War wooden caricature by the noted artist Edward Carter Preston. Preston also designed Great War military medals and plaques to honor the fallen. He created Churchill in 1915 as part of his *Men Who Matter* series, and utilized his unique process of sealing layers of wood together prior to carving them. The series was designed to be reproduced in templates which could then be constructed by recuperating soldiers at the Lord Roberts homes.

First Lord of the Admiralty – Colonial Secretary – MP for Epping 1911-1924

Churchill is included among the British and Allied leaders pictured on this large silk textile made in the early days of the Great War. They all surround the famous "Scrap of Paper" illustrated in the middle. In 1839, the Treaty of London, signed by Great Britain, France, Russia, Austria, and Germany declared Belgium an independent, neutral state. On 3 August 1914, Great Britain sent an ultimatum to Germany to not invade Belgium. The next day, German troops invaded Belgium and Great Britain declared war. When reminded of the Treaty of London, the German Chancellor referred to it as a "scrap of paper." The "scrap of paper" was a popular theme and rallying cry of British wartime propaganda as proof that Germany reneged on the treaty and could not be trusted.

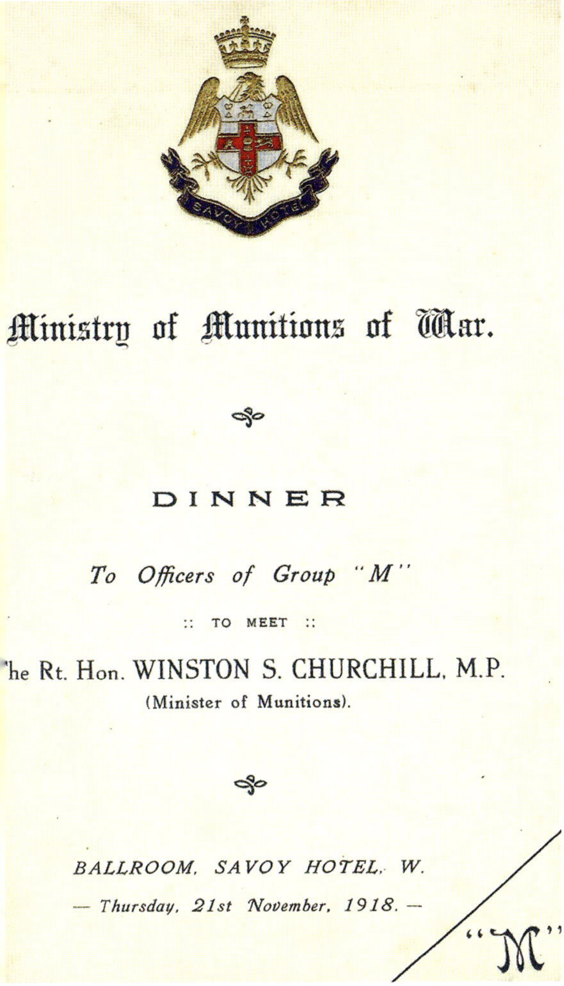

Ministry of Munitions of War.

DINNER

To Officers of Group "M"

:: TO MEET ::

The Rt. Hon. WINSTON S. CHURCHILL, M.P.
(Minister of Munitions).

BALLROOM, SAVOY HOTEL, W.
— Thursday, 21st November, 1918. —

"M"

Material from Churchill's service as Minister of Munitions in Lloyd George's coalition government is difficult to find. This 21 November 1918 program for a dinner held in the ballroom of London's Savoy Hotel is a fine survivor.

This postcard shows a candid image of Churchill campaigning for re-election to the House of Commons for Dundee during the 1918 General Election. This was the first general election called since the Great War began four years earlier.

As Secretary of State for War and Air, Winston Churchill visited the British Army of Occupation at Cologne, Germany on 19 August 1919. A formal review of troops was held at Cathedral Square. Later that day, Churchill visited members of the all female Queen Mary's Auxiliary Corps. Serving in France, Belgium and Germany both during and after the Great War, these women took on such tasks as cooking, first aid, clerical and administrative work and motor vehicle maintenance.

First Lord of the Admiralty – Colonial Secretary – MP for Epping 1911-1924

CHAPTER FOUR

Chancellor of the Exchequer – Return to Admiralty 1924-1939

This chapter covers the period 1924- 1939, from Churchill's service as Chancellor of the Exchequer in the Baldwin government through his return as First Lord of the Admiralty the day Prime Minister Chamberlain declared war on Germany. In between these two important positions, there is a time referred to as Churchill's "Wilderness Years." During that time, he was still MP for Epping but held no cabinet appointment. He had detractors on both sides of the aisle in the House of Commons as well as among the public.

Given the importance of the office, historical items exist from Churchill's tenure as Chancellor of the Exchequer. In fact, the very first Toby jug of Churchill was made during his time as Chancellor and it is illustrated in this chapter. Likewise, Churchill's popularity had risen by the time he was appointed back as First Lord of the Admiralty in the Chamberlain government. Within this chapter are beautiful porcelain pieces made to commemorate his return to the Admiralty.

Likewise, the term "Wilderness Years" has been considered a misnomer by many, as it implies that Churchill was wondering aimlessly without direction. This is not true. It refers to his time without a cabinet position, although he was still MP for Epping with increasing majorities each election. Churchill used this time to work on his Kent estate, Chartwell, to write books and articles for profit and to speak out in Parliament about the rising German threat of war and Britain's need to be prepared. Churchill's "Wilderness Years" were focused and busy; material exists from his various public appearances and speaking engagements.

As with every chapter, the brief synopsis of this timed period is followed by illustrations and descriptions of historical pieces.

On 6 November 1924, after being out of Parliament for two years, Churchill was appointed Chancellor of the Exchequer in Stanley Baldwin's Conservative government. He rejoined the Conservative Party the same day. He would remain Chancellor of the Exchequer until the 1929 general election in which the Conservatives were defeated and Ramsay MacDonald formed his second Labour government. Churchill presented five budgets through April, 1929. In his first budget in 1925, he returned Britain to the gold standard against the advice of many leading economists. The return to gold was said to be the cause of deflation and resulting unemployment, particularly within Britain's coal industry. His subsequent budgets included a reduction of the pension age from 70 to 65, pensions for war widows, reductions of military expenditures, income tax reductions and a new tax on luxury goods.

Britain experienced a nine-day general strike, 3-13 May 1926, which included a nationwide work stoppage called by the Trade Union Council. The strike showed solidarity and support of Britain's striking coal miners. During the strike, Churchill edited the *British Gazette*, the government's anti-strike propaganda newspaper and was ever disliked by Britain's trade unions. After the strike ended, he worked with Labour's Ramsay MacDonald as an intermediary between striking miners and their employers to find solutions to workers' grievances. As a result, Churchill called for the introduction of a legally binding minimum wage.

In the Spring of 1927, Churchill began yet another interest, bricklaying. His garden walls and children's playhouse can be seen at Chartwell today. He used to jokingly boast he could lay "200 bricks and 2000 words a day."

In September, 1928, he joined the Amalgamated Union of Building Trade Workers as a brick mason.

In the 30 May 1929 general election, Churchill retained his seat as MP for Epping, but the Baldwin Conservative government was defeated. Ramsay MacDonald formed his second Labour government with Liberal support. Churchill resigned as Chancellor of the Exchequer on June 4, and began what is referred to as his "Wilderness Years," 1929-1939.

Out of office, Churchill felt his political talents were being wasted. Writing proved cathartic. He began work on *Marlborough: His Life and Times*, the four-volume biography of his ancestor John Churchill, 1st Duke of Marlborough. In October 1930, after his return from a trip to North America, Churchill published his autobiography, *My Early Life*, which was well received by the public.

In January 1931, Churchill resigned from the Conservative Shadow Cabinet because Stanley Baldwin supported the decision of MacDonald's Labour government to support the India Act, which would grant Dominion status to India. Churchill believed such status would eventually lead to calls for full independence. Similarly, he publicly criticized Mohandas Gandhi. While his views were supported by many Conservatives, they were not at all well received by members of the Labour and Liberal parties.

In the October 1931 general election, Churchill almost doubled his support in Epping. The election was a landslide victory for the Conservative party itself. Despite the Conservative victory, Churchill was not given a ministerial position. The India Act and Dominion status for India continued to be debated into December in the House of Commons. Later that month, Churchill left for a lecture tour of North America, hoping to recoup financial losses suffered in the 1929 American stock market crash. On 13 December, he was struck by a car while crossing Fifth Avenue in New York City. As a result, he suffered a head wound and neuritis. After being discharged from the hospital, he recuperated in Nassau for three weeks, accompanied by his wife, Clementine. He returned to America in January, 1932 and resumed his lecture tour, which included Hartford, Springfield, Boston, St. Louis, New

York, Atlanta, New Orleans, Richmond, and Toronto. He returned home to Britain on 18 March.

After Hitler was elected Chancellor of Germany on 20 January 1933, Chartwell became a base for intelligence gathering and privileged discussion. Guests providing Churchill with confidential information and opinions typically did not sign the visitors' book. These informants included British government officials, former German government officials, French officials and military officers. The Baldwin government was aware of Churchill's information gathering and publicly feigned outrage.

On 14 March 1933, Churchill gave his first speech in the House of Commons warning of the need to rebuild Britain's air defenses. Armed with official data confidentially provided by two senior government officers, Churchill was able to speak with authority about Germany's development of the Luftwaffe. In February, 1934 Churchill again brought Germany's war production to the attention of the House of Commons in a speech outlining their naval build-up and Britain's corresponding need for maintenance of Fleet strength. He also warned of German shadow factories that could be quickly converted to war production. On 2 August 1934, upon the death of Von Hindenburg, Hitler proclaimed himself both Chancellor and Fuhrer. Churchill continued to denounce Nazism in the House of Commons and in November, 1934, shared his concerns with the public in a radio broadcast.

In February, 1935, the House of Commons passed the India Act. Churchill and 83 other Conservative MPs voted against it. In June 1935, Ramsey MacDonald resigned as Prime Minister and was replaced by Conservative Stanley Baldwin. The same month, under the Baldwin government, Britain and Germany entered the Anglo-German Naval Agreement, which allowed Germany to possess up to 35% of British naval strength. Germany would soon disregard the limit and produced U-boats and other naval vessels far exceeding the agreed upon limits. Churchill continued to speak publicly on the necessity of building Britain's air defenses. In July, he joined the Air Defense Research subcommittee of the Committee for Imperial Defense with the approval of the Secretary of State for Air and Baldwin himself. While serving on the committee, Churchill was still free to argue his position of the need to increase Britain's air defenses before the House of Commons. On 14 November 1935, the Conservative Party won a majority in the 1935 general election. Churchill retained his seat in Epping with yet another increased majority but was not asked to join the Baldwin government.

On 20 January 1936, King George V died and was succeeded by his son, Edward VIII. His desire to marry an American divorcee, Wallis Simpson, caused an abdication crisis. Churchill supported Edward and publicly clashed with Baldwin on the issue. On 7 December, Churchill was shouted down and ruled out of order in the House of Commons when he spoke in favor of Edward VIII remaining king. Edward abdicated on 10 December and was succeeded by his brother, George VI. Churchill immediately pledged loyalty to the new king, although later writing abdication was not necessary.

In May 1937, Baldwin resigned and Neville Chamberlain succeeded him as Prime Minister. At first, Churchill welcomed Chamberlain's appointment but, in February 1938, was critical of the Prime Minister's appeasement of Mussolini, which prompted the resignation of Foreign Secretary Anthony Eden. Churchill continued to offer public criticism when Chamberlain also extended appeasement to Hitler. In 1938, Churchill spoke in the House of Commons against appeasement and contended collective action was necessary to thwart German aggression. In March, the *Evening Standard* stopped publishing Churchill's articles, but they soon appeared in the *Daily Telegraph*. Following the German annexation of Austria, Churchill again spoke in the House of Commons, maintaining the seriousness of events. He began calling for a mutual defense pact among European states threatened by German expansionism, arguing collectively there was a chance to stop Hitler. No action was taken and in September, Germany mobilized to invade the Sudetenland in Czechoslovakia. Churchill urged Chamberlain to tell Germany that Britain would declare war if the Germans invaded Czechoslovak territory; Chamberlain ignored Churchill's advice. Instead, on 30 September, Chamberlain and Hitler signed the Munich Agreement. Chamberlain returned to Britain and publicly declared "Peace in our time." The Munich Agreement allowed the German annexation of the Sudetenland. Hitler promised to support Czech independence. Speaking in the House of Commons on 5 October, Churchill predicted that Hitler would soon annex Czechoslovakia. Few MPs sided with Churchill. Following the German invasion and annexation of Czechoslovakia on 4 March 1939, Churchill and his supporters called for a national coalition. Given current events, Churchill's popularity increased and people began to call for his return to office.

Poland was next to be threatened by Hitler's advancement. On 31 March, Britain guaranteed Poland's independence. Hitler invaded Poland on 1 September. On 2 September, France began mobilizing for war. On 3 September, Britain and France declared war on Germany; the same day, Chamberlain returned Churchill to the position of First Lord of the Admiralty and a member of the war cabinet.

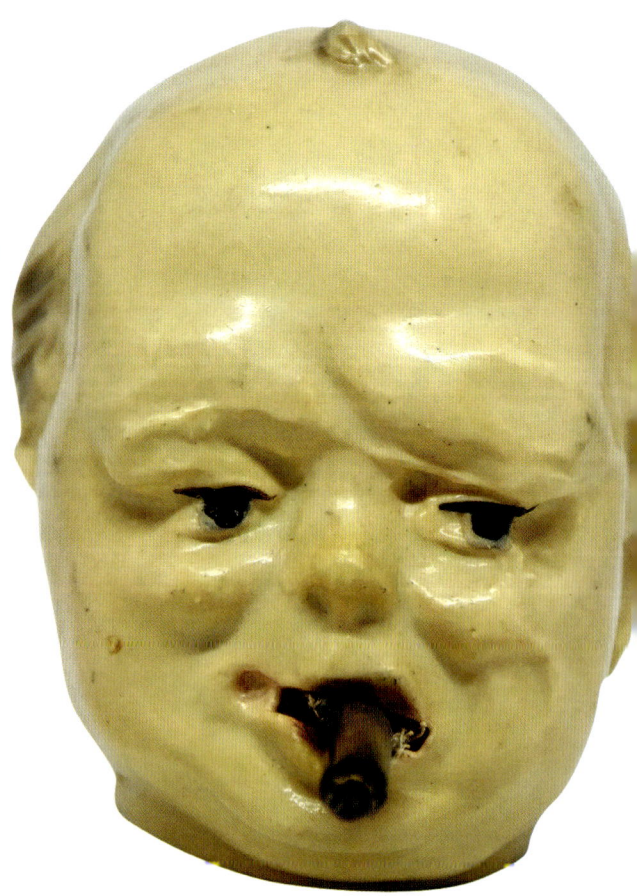

Only two inches in height and made of celluloid, WSC's head contains a cloth, spring wound tape measure which is extended by pulling on his cigar. The piece dates to 1924-1929 when Churchill served as Chancellor of the Exchequer. Similar tape measures molded as the heads of Prime Ministers Stanley Baldwin and David Lloyd George were also produced.

David Low was publicly praised by Churchill as being Britain's greatest editorial cartoonist. Low's illustration of Churchill as Chancellor of the Exchequer was published in the *Evening Standard* in 1926 as one in a series of illustrations of 32 prominent men of the day. The Low illustrations could be purchased from the newspaper as individual prints.

CITY OF NOTTINGHAM
CONSERVATIVE ASSOCIATION.
PRESIDENT — SIR JAMES W. McCRAITH, J.P.

□ o □

MASS MEETING

ADDRESS
BY

THE RIGHT HON. WINSTON CHURCHILL, M.P.,
IN THE
ALBERT HALL, NOTTINGHAM,
FRIDAY, 21ST OCTOBER, 1927, AT 8 P.M.

7.20 P.M.   PANATROPE CONCERT.

This blotter was made by the City of Nottingham Conservative Association as a souvenir of Churchill's address to their mass meeting on 21 October 1927. Churchill's address was preceded by a demonstration of the newly invented Panatrope, an electric phonograph.

This postcard featuring a confident Chancellor Churchill was produced and sold by Woolworth's in their London stores.

This well-executed plaster bust dates to Churchill's time as Chancellor of the Exchequer. For centuries, British statesmen have been the subject of these types of items, including the Chancellor of the Exchequer.

Made by W.H. Goss in 1927, this is the very first Toby jug ever created in the likeness of Winston Churchill. It was made when Churchill was Chancellor of the Exchequer. In 1926, Churchill introduced a tax on betting that proved to be very unpopular. The jug depicts him seated with his hands together in prayer. He's wearing a top hat inscribed *Any odds bar one. That's me who kissed the Blarney Stone*. The jug is found with Churchill wearing either a blue or green coat. Interestingly, there is no historical support for Churchill ever kissing the Blarney Stone.

Chancellor of the Exchequer – Return to Admiralty 1924-1939

Rt. Honourable Winston S. Churchill

Famous British Statesman

THE Pittsburgh Morning Lecture Series management regards it a great honor to announce the only public appearance in Pittsburgh of the Right Honourable Winston Spencer Churchill, "the stormy petrel of British politics." Grandson of a Duke of Marlborough, son of Lord Randolph Churchill and Jennie Jerome of Baltimore and New York (Lady Randolph Churchill), Winston Churchill was born to the purple, brought up in an atmosphere of politics and statecraft, and before he had reached his thirties was launched upon a spectacular career, that is still in the making a quarter of a century later.

Recently, the American Vanity Fair printed a short appreciation of the many sided Churchill, written by the British author, Harold Nicolson, which we reprint here:

"Winston Churchill is the most interesting man in England. He is more than interesting; he is a phenomenon, an enigma. How can a man so versatile and so brilliant avoid being considered volatile and unsound? He will live in English history long after those who have made it are forgotten, for he is an Anglo-American freak, and England loves her freaks devotedly (once they are safely dead).

"Before he was twenty-six, he had seen more fighting than the oldest general. He was a Member of Parliament before he was twenty-seven, a Member of the Ministry before he was thirty-one, and a full-blown Cabinet Minister at thirty-four. Since then, he has been Minister of Commerce, Colonies, Navy, Munitions, Home Affairs, War, Air, and Treasury.

"He devised the Antwerp and the Dardanelles campaigns, and it was not his fault that they failed. He adopted the device of tanks for trench warfare, and it was not his fault that they were used too soon. It is largely to him that the Irish settlement is to be attributed.

"He is the best living writer of English narrative prose. He is a landscape painter superior to most academicians. He can do anything from playing polo to brick-laying.

"His dominant qualities are imagination, courage and loyalty; his dominant defect, impatience. He is a man who leads forlorn hopes, and when the hopes of England become forlorn, he will once again be summoned to leadership."

As an orator of brilliant attainments, Mr. Churchill has world-wide fame. In a singular degree, he has the dramatic sense and the gift of eloquence. His style is vivid, terse, lively, and scintillating with wit.

At Eight O'Clock
Monday Evening, March 7th

Subject:
"The Pathway of English-Speaking Peoples"

[7]

CHURCHILL'S POLITICAL CAREER

Some of the political posts that have been held by the Rt. Hon. Winston Spencer Churchill are:

1. Member of Parliament for Twenty-Five years.
2. Chance 1924-29
3. Ministe
4. Secreta 1918-21
5. Ministe
6. Lord I versity.
7. First 1911-1[?]
8. Home
9. Presid 1908-1[?]
10. Under 1906-0[?]

On 7 March 1932, Churchill spoke at Oakland's Carnegie Music Hall as part of the Pittsburgh Lecture Series. Churchill was visiting the United States, hoping a series of speaking engagements would help recoup his financial losses caused by the 1929 stock market crash. At the time of his lecture, Churchill was out of government but still a brilliant and popular speaker.

In his speech, he stressed the importance of maintaining a strong military and the joint role the United States and Great Britain played in promoting world peace.

78 - A Churchill Treasury

During the years between the Great War and Second World War, Churchill warned the British people of Germany's disregard for the armament limitations imposed by the Treaty of Versailles. On 16 November, 1934, he gave what many consider one of his greatest speeches of this period. Simply titled *The Causes of War*, the speech was broadcast live via the BBC. Churchill emphasized the major threat to peace was "a nation which with all its strength and virtues is in the grip of a group of ruthless men preaching a gospel of intolerance and racial pride, unrestrained by law." The speech was printed verbatim in the BBC's written publication, *The Listener*, on 21 November. This large poster is a rare survivor and would have been used at newsstands to attract customers interested in reading Churchill's recent speech.

Chancellor of the Exchequer – Return to Admiralty 1924-1939

WESTERHAM 93.

CHARTWELL,
WESTERHAM,
KENT.

June 17 1939

Dear Mr. Joseph,

        I thought you might be interested to know that I have rather a good job here in the country as Private Secretary to Mr. Winston Churchill. I have been here nearly two months now and like it very much indeed. It should interest you to know that in applying for the post I produced that wonderful testimonial which you wrote for me when I left the Theatre. So I feel grateful to you.

        I thought - much as I loved the work! - that the hours at the Theatre were long, but they were as nothing compared with these! I start at 9.30 in the morning and seldom, if ever, finish before 2.0 the next morning! Mr. Churchill likes dictating his books after dinner at night and has the most amazing energy - a very likely rival to your own unbounded energy!

        There are two of us - secretaries, I mean - so we take things in turns and as my colleague likes to be at home during the week-ends, I take equivalent time off during the week - which I much prefer. One of us has to be here all the time, so its very fortunate that we each like a different time off.

        The work is most frightfully interesting and - though you may not have known it! - working at high pressure is most exhilirating to me, so that it is most suitable! Of course Mr. Churchill is in Town a good deal, in the House - and we rush back and forth from here - mostly working in the car on the way.

        I hope everything is going well with you - now and then I have come to Town by Green Line Coach and passed the Lewisham Hippodrome and often thought I would like to pop in and see you.

        Best wishes and many thanks for that useful piece of your hand-writing!

        Sincerely,

Mary S.G. Shearburn

On 17 June 1939, Ms. Mary Shearborn wrote to her former employer, assuring him that she had found a good job as private secretary to Mr. Winston Churchill. This letter, typed on Chartwell letterhead, was written during Churchill's "wilderness years" and describes a typical day in his employ. Ms. Shearborn continued working as Churchill's private secretary through the war and in 1945, married his bodyguard, Inspector Thompson. We must add *matchmaker* to the long list of Churchill's impressive titles and accomplishments.

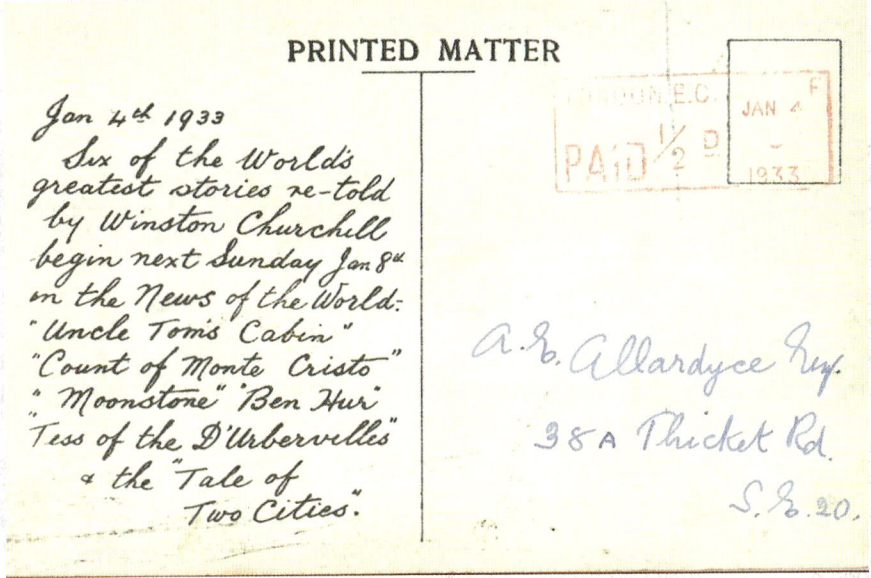

During his "Wilderness Years," Churchill stayed busy by focusing on his primary occupation as a writer. In 1933, while commissioned to write numerous newspaper articles, Churchill was also responsible for writing a 12-part series for *The News of the World* entitled *The World's Greatest Stories*. For each part, Churchill retold a literary classic. His secretary, Eddie Marsh, prepared a synopsis of each plot as the foundation for Churchill's subsequent retelling.

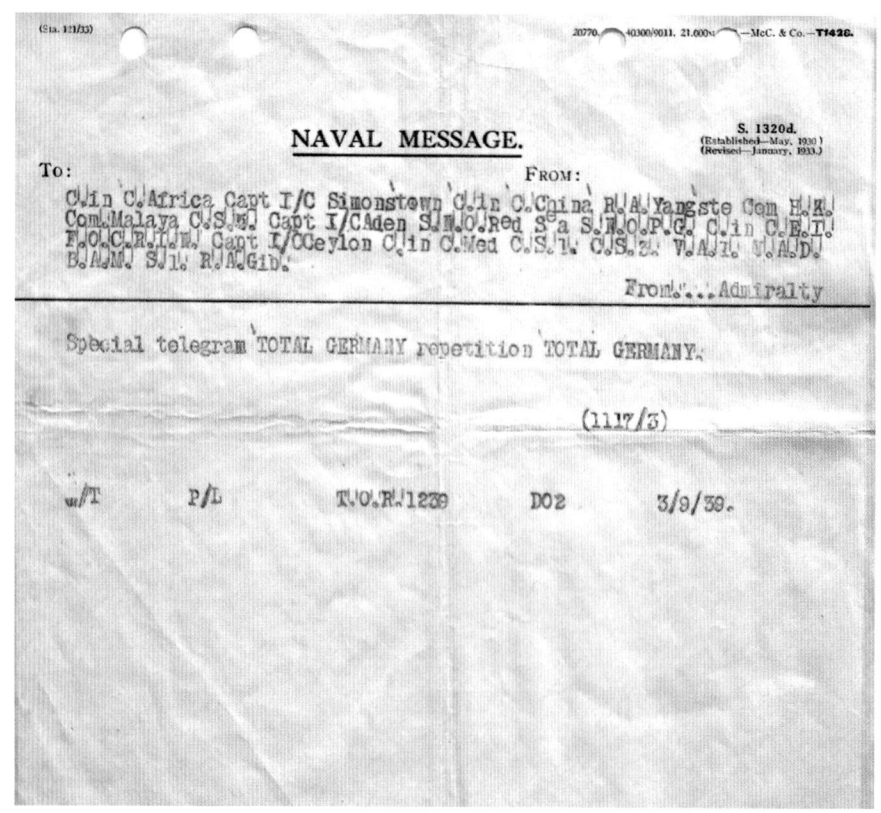

As the new First Lord of the Admiralty in Neville Chamberlain's war cabinet, one of Churchill's very first tasks on 3 September 1939 was to send these telegrams. One was sent to the fleet and the other was sent to the colonies, alerting them that Britain had declared war on Germany.

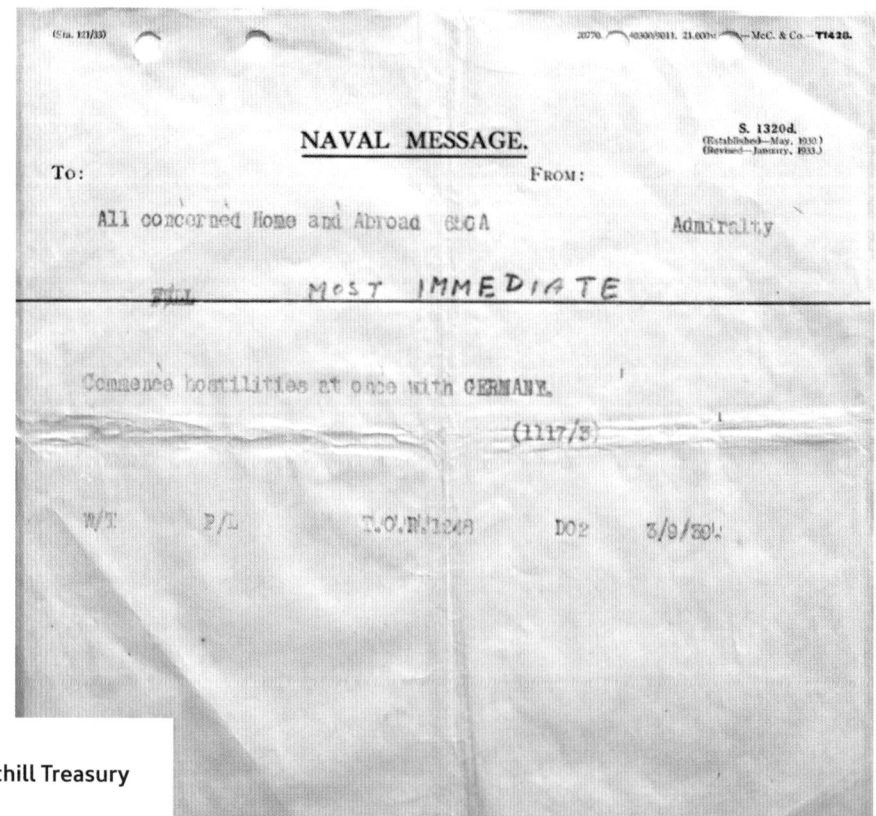

When Churchill returned as First Lord of the Admiralty on 2 September 1939, porcelain and pottery manufacturers wasted no time in commemorating the occasion. Some prime examples include:

• *Winston the Winner*, showing a smiling Churchill in a naval uniform, with a cigar, telescope and bulldog, 1939, chalkware, maanufacturer unknown;

• Churchill astride the battleship *Winston*, 1939, chalkware, manufacturer unknown;

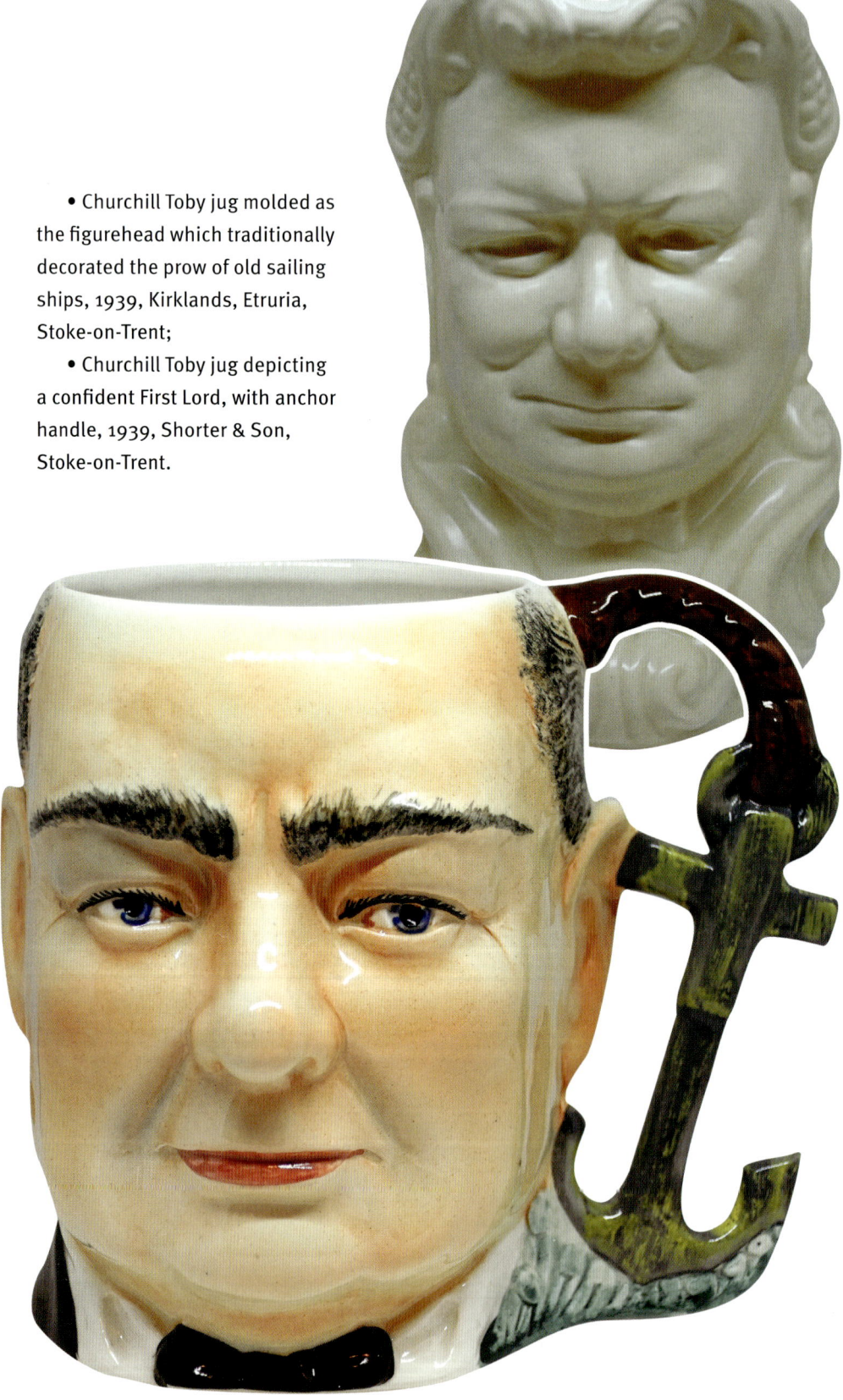

- Churchill Toby jug molded as the figurehead which traditionally decorated the prow of old sailing ships, 1939, Kirklands, Etruria, Stoke-on-Trent;
- Churchill Toby jug depicting a confident First Lord, with anchor handle, 1939, Shorter & Son, Stoke-on-Trent.

CHAPTER FIVE

World War II – The First Premiership

What follows is a brief historical timeline of Winston Churchill's first premiership, 1940-1945. It is by no means designed to be a fully documented history of the Second World War. Rather, this timeline is to be used as a guide to place the historical items pictured in this chapter into a corresponding framework. This era was the pinnacle time period for the production and manufacture of Churchill material, as one would expect. Indeed, this includes a vast array of manufactured items, including porcelain, clay, wood, paper, glass, metal and textiles. Likewise, they also include many pieces of wartime handmade folk art. The historical materials presented in this chapter are sorted by Prime Minister Churchill's numerous wartime travels and events. Please enjoy viewing them as you make your way through the history they represent.

On 10 May 1940, Germany invaded Belgium, France, Luxembourg and the Netherlands. This led to the resignation of Neville Chamberlain. In turn, Winston Churchill became Prime Minister of the United Kingdom and was called on to form a wartime coalition government. On 13 May, he delivered his memorable "Blood, Toil, Tears and Sweat" speech before the House of Commons. The next day, 14 May 1940, Churchill's coalition government, comprised of Conservatives, Labour and Liberal members, was made public. Also, on this day, Churchill sought wartime aid from the United States and Canada. Later that month, on 30 May 1940, during a critical meeting of the wartime coalition cabinet, Churchill won a vote on continuing the war rather than seeking an appeased peace as proposed by Lord Halifax and former Prime Minister Chamberlain.

The month of June, 1940 is noteworthy for the delivery of two of Churchill's most remembered speeches. On 4 June 1940, he delivered his " We Shall Fight on the Beaches..." speech before the House of Commons. On 18 June 1940, he delivered his famous "Finest Hour" speech, again before the House of Commons.

The Battle of Britain commenced on 10 July 1940 and would continue through 31 October. On 20 August, Churchill delivered his iconic "The Few" speech before the House of Commons. On 25 August, Churchill ordered the bombing of Berlin in response to German aerial attacks on Britain. The Blitz commenced on 7 September and lasted until 11 May 1941. On 9 October 1940, Neville Chamberlain resigned from the House of Commons due to ill health. Upon his resignation, Churchill was elected head of the Conservative Party.

In December 1940, President Franklin D. Roosevelt first proposed Lend-Lease in attempt to provide Great Britain necessary aid by maneuvering around the United States' existing isolationist policies. Under Lend-Lease, the United States would lend, rather than sell, military supplies to Great Britain for use in the fight against Germany. Of course, there was strong opposition among isolationist members of Congress. On 29 December 1940, during one of his "fireside chats," Roosevelt declared "We must be the great arsenal of democracy..."

On 9 February 1941, Churchill delivered his famous "Give Us the Tools" speech in support of Lend-Lease. One month later, Congress passed the Lend-Lease Act and Roosevelt signed it into law on 11 March. Roosevelt quickly ordered large quantities of American food and war materials shipped to Britain.

On 19 July 1941, the "V-sign", famously associated with Churchill, was unofficially adopted as the Allied victory symbol. A month later, from 9 to 12 August, Roosevelt and Churchill held their Atlantic Charter conference aboard naval ships in Placentia Bay, off the southeast coast of Newfoundland. It was the first time the two leaders had met as heads of their respective governments. They met under utmost secrecy and without any press coverage to avoid the threat of German U-Boat attacks or criticism by American isolationists. The meeting was not disclosed to the public until the Atlantic Charter was signed on 14 August. The Atlantic Charter was a declaration of universal freedoms and its signing is considered the first effort toward establishing the United Nations in 1945.

7 December 1941 witnessed the attack by Japan on the US naval base and Pacific fleet at Pearl Harbor, Hawaii. When Churchill was notified of the attack in a phone call from President Roosevelt, he was at Chequers in the company of the President's special envoy, Averell Harriman, and the US Ambassador to Britain, John Gilbert Winant. The next day, 8 December, Japan attacked Hong Kong, Malaya and the Philippines. Later the same month Churchill traveled to Washington, DC as a guest of President Roosevelt; on 26 December, he delivered his first address to a joint session of Congress. Later that evening, while in the White House, he suffered a mild heart attack that remained undisclosed to all but his traveling party which included his personal physician.

Churchill's next visit to the United States was in June, 1942. He arrived on 18 June and began meetings with President Roosevelt. This visit, known as the Second Washington Conference, would last until 25 June. It was more of a meeting amongst military staff rather than a traditional, formal conference between the heads of state. Discussions included how the Western Allies could best aid the Soviet Union. Also, an agreement was reached to begin preparations for Operation Torch, the allied invasion of North Africa. Part of the planning for Operation Torch included President Roosevelt appointing General Dwight D. Eisenhower as Commander in Chief of American Forces in the European Theatre. Lastly, Roosevelt and Churchill also held discussions with members of the Pacific War Council.

On 2 July 1942: Churchill and his coalition government survived a censure motion in the House of Commons. The motion was brought because Britian had suffered a series of military defeats. When the vote was taken, Churchill's government was supported by 475 votes to 25.

From 14 to 24 January 1943, Roosevelt and Churchill convened the Casablanca Conference to discuss the impending invasion of Sicily and Italy, the eventual invasion of mainland Europe and the ramifications of "unconditional surrender" by Germany.

From 12 to 25 May 1943, the Third Washington Conference convened to discuss the Allied invasion of Sicily, the date for invading Normandy, and the progress of the Pacific War. Churchill and Roosevelt met every two days in the White House, while British and American military leaders met daily. On 19 May, Churchill delivered his second address before a joint session of Congress, praising the partnership of Great Britain and the United States and declaring that the war would continue until tyranny was destroyed.

From 17 to 24 August 1943, the First Quebec Conference was held in Quebec City and was attended by the allied leaders of the United States, Great Britain and Canada. This was a highly secret military conference which included discussions for the planning of the invasion of France, codenamed Operation Overlord. There were discussions about improving the coordination of efforts by the Americans, British, and Canadians to develop an atomic bomb. Churchill and Roosevelt, without Canadian input, signed the Quebec Agreement, stating that nuclear technology would never be used against one another, nor against third parties without the consent of one another.

The next conference of allied leaders was held in Cairo, Egypt, 22-27 November 1943 and included President Roosevelt, Prime Minister Churchill and Republic of China leader Chiang Kai-shek. The primary discussion concerned the defeat of Japan. The Conference ended with the signing of the Cairo Declaration, which set forth the intent to win the war in the Pacific. The Tehran Conference began the following day, attended by Roosevelt, Churchill and Soviet Premiere Joseph Stalin. The primary focus of this conference was to discuss European war strategy. On 30 November, they completed the preliminary Operation Overlord planning. On 4 December 1943, a second Cairo Conference was held. This time, Roosevelt and Churchill met with Mustafa Ismet Inonu of Turkey.

On 6 June 1944 Operation Overlord was executed, and British, Canadian and US troops landed at Normandy in France and initiated a second front against Germany. 6 June is forever known as D-Day.

Only days later, beginning 13 June, London came under heavy attack again by pilotless V-1 and V-2 rockets, which were fired from Nazi-occupied Europe. The attacks ended when the launching sites were captured in October. Of the approximately 10,000 rockets launched against England, 2,419 reached London. 6,184 people were killed and 17,981 were injured.

On 20 August 1944, Allied troops reached Paris and the city was liberated five days later. In November, Churchill travelled to France for the anniversary of the Great War armistice. The Prime Minister and General de Gaulle together laid a wreath at the Tomb of the Unknown Soldier at the Arc de Triomphe.

The Second Quebec Conference was held 12-16 September 1944. Held in Quebec City, the conference allowed Roosevelt and Churchill to discuss military cooperation in the Pacific and the future of Germany. Agreements were reached concerning allied occupation zones in defeated Germany, the demilitarization of Germany, continued U.S. Lend-Lease aid to Britain, and the role of the Royal Navy in the war against Japan.

The Moscow Conference was held the following month, 9-19 October 1944. Roosevelt was not present at this conference. Rather, Churchill and Stalin discussed spheres of influence in postwar Europe. Churchill made a secret written proposal to divide postwar Europe into Western and Soviet spheres of influence. After reviewing Churchill's proposal, Stalin agreed by writing a large check in blue pencil and returning the paper to Churchill. This came to be known as the "Percentages Agreement".

The Yalta Conference was held 4 to 11 February 1945 near Yalta in the Crimea. Attended by Roosevelt, Churchill and Stalin, the main discussions concerned the unconditional surrender of Germany and dividing the country into postwar spheres of influence. After the war, Germany and Berlin itself would be split into four occupied zones. Stalin agreed that France would have a fourth occupation zone in Germany if it was formed from the American and the British zones. The parties also agreed that Nazi war criminals were to be found and put on trial in the territories in which their crimes had been committed. Nazi leaders were to be executed.

Yalta would be the last allied conference attended by President Roosevelt. On 12 April 1945, he died after suffering a cerebral hemorrhage while at his home in Warm Springs, Georgia. He was succeeded by Vice President Harry S. Truman. Four days later, on 16 April 1945, Soviet forces overtook Berlin. Hitler committed suicide 30 April and was succeeded by Karl Doenitz.

On 7 May, Germany surrendered to the western Allies. On 8 May, Churchill broadcast to the nation that the war with Germany had been won. He then joined King George VI and the royal family on the balcony of Buckingham Palace and waved to crowds at Whitehall.

On 23 May 1945, Churchill's wartime coalition government was dissolved and replaced by a caretaker government. Shortly thereafter, on 5 June 1945, the longest parliament of the 20th century was dissolved.

On 17 July 1945, the Potsdam Conference began under Churchill (later replaced by his successor, Clement Attlee), Stalin and Truman. The Allied leaders agreed to insist upon the unconditional surrender of Japan, which took place on 9 August 1945.

On 26 July 1945, the Labour Party won the United Kingdom's general election by a landslide. Churchill resigned as Prime Minister. His first premiership had ended.

WINSTON CHURCHILL WARTIME PORCELAIN ITEMS

Given that Britain has been a center for porcelain manufacturing for at least four centuries, it's no surprise that the tradition of making commemoratives included Churchill. Early in the war, the porcelain manufacturers were requisitioned by the government for the production of wartime necessities. Later, though, that restriction was modified to allow the manufacture of wartime commemoratives. Shown here is a representative sampling of the wartime porcelain items produced by many of Britain's best known and well established porcelain houses.

Clarice Cliff was one of Great Britain's most famous ceramic artists and designers. Beginning in 1930, she became the art director for Newport Pottery. Her designs of colorfully patterned tableware were popular in the 1930s and remain sought after by collectors today. In the early 1940s, Ms. Cliff also designed and produced three pieces depicting Winston Churchill, which like her other works, are highly sought. First, the Toby jug seen here is considered the best of the wartime-produced Churchill jugs. It was initially designed in 1915 to be part of the Great War Wilkinson set, but was excluded after his resignation as First Lord of the Admiralty. Thankfully, the design was archived and remembered after Churchill became Prime Minister. After Ms. Cliff revised the jug's design, it was issued for Christmas, 1941 sales in a limited edition of 350 and offered exclusively through Harrods.

She also designed and produced this large colorful charger of Churchill, utilizing his "Let Us Go Forward Together" phrase; he initially used this phrase in a 1928 budget broadcast as Chancellor of the Exchequer. He utilized it again in his wartime speeches in 1940 as First Lord of the Admiralty and as Prime Minister in 1941-1945. Lastly, the porcelain figurine of Churchill is well executed and popular amongst collectors.

Pictured here are two fine representatives of the many plates featuring the Prime Minister that were produced during WW2. First, the plate with patriotic motif comes in both red and blue and was made by Burgess & Leigh in 1941. Next, the square plate with raised Florentine border was made by Crown Ducal in 1940. The sepia transfer image of Churchill is titled "The Fighting Premiere" and is from a photograph by Cecil Beaton.

The venerable Royal Doulton manufactured some beautiful wartime pieces. First, the set of three Toby jugs was first produced in 1940 to commemorate Churchill's becoming Prime Minister. This was the first and only run of these marked "Prime

Minister" on the bottom.
The set proved to be one of
Royal Doulton's best sellers and was made into
the 1980s. All subsequent sets are marked "Winston Churchill." Next, Royal
Doulton produced this wonderful porcelain box containing small tray inserts, each
bearing a different Churchill quotation. The transfer pattern on the lid was also
utilized on mugs, plates and other items. Lastly, the Royal Doulton bulldog is a
take on Churchill as it smokes a cigar and wears one of his favorite hats.

World War II – The First Premiership - 95

Utilityware is the term given to the wartime everyday porcelain produced for British domestic use. Although solidly made and collectible today, it not of the caliber of porcelain made by the premiere manufacturers. Typically, utilityware is white and bears the same brown transfer image of Churchill. These two pieces, a teacup and saucer and a pitcher, are nice representatives of the plates, bowls, platters and other utilityware pieces made during wartime.

This wonderfully designed and painted bone china figurine of Winston Churchill was made by WT Copeland/Spode in 1941.

It's obvious who Crown Devon was thinking of when producing this porcelain bulldog. Note the "V's" on the paws.

World War II – The First Premiership

Cooper Clayton

The original Toby jugs were created by Staffordshire potters in the 1760s and had a brown salt glaze. Over time, the jugs have been manufactured by numerous British porcelain makers and are an iconic product of the industry. Upon Winston Churchill becoming prime minister on 10 May 1940, several of the British porcelain manufacturers sought to honor him by making commemorative Toby jugs. Some were cheaply produced and bear a questionable likeness, while others were finely made and capture Churchill's facial features very nicely. Pictured here is a representative sampling of Churchill Toby jugs produced 1940-1945.

Avon Ware

Burgess & Leigh

Burleighware

Lancaster's Hanley

World War II – The First Premiership

Sandlandware

Wilton

(Unmarked)

(Unmarked)

Wilton

World War II – The First Premiership

This beautiful Toby jug was produced by Medalta of Canada in 1940 to honour Churchill becoming Prime Minister. It incorporates the legendary message from his 4 June 1940 speech, "We Shall Not Flag or Fail."

Meakin

Royal Winton

This Beswick Toby is usually found without the top head portion. Given its precarious nature, the head has fallen off and been damaged on most examples that come to market.

Falconware produced this clever and well designed wartime piece. Churchill's hat is a removable ashtray which sits atop a tobacco jar.

This nicely hand painted, high relief porcelain box contains a set of small tray inserts. The inside lid includes a paper label verifying it was produced in 1941 by Lancaster & Sons under wartime conditions.

World War II – The First Premiership

Bakelite was an early form of plastic, used during the Second World War in the manufacture of war materials and household goods. These medallions featuring the Prime Minister were offered in two colour schemes and were designed to hang on a wall or adorn a shelf or mantelpiece.

"After hours ware" describes a genre of pieces made "off the clock" by company employees from surplus or scrap materials they have on hand in their workplace. Offered here are three prime examples. The tiled dish would have been made by someone in the tile, masonry or plumbing trade; the back is made of terra cotta earthenware used in all three trades. The wall plaque was carved by an employee of the Canadian Pacific Railway on a piece of scrap wood likely found in a rail yard.

Lastly, the ashtray was made from scrap airplane aluminum by employees of the British based DeHavilland Aircraft Company, who sold them as fundraisers for various wartime benevolent funds.

World War II – The First Premiership

The story of how and why this wartime plaster bust of Prime Minister Winston Churchill was produced by noted sculptress Barbara Tribe is fascinating.

The sculptress, Barbara Tribe, immigrated from Sydney, Australia to London in 1935. In London, she became a member of the Royal Academy and worked as an in-house sculptress at Selfridges, creating commissioned busts for the department store's wealthy customers. She also maintained her own studio.

Shortly after war was declared, Ms. Tribe went to work for the Ministry of Supply. In 1942, she was recruited by the newly created Inspectorate of Ancient Monuments, which was tasked with documenting London's major landmarks to determine whether blitz damage necessitated restoration work. In this capacity, Ms. Tribe informally met the Prime Minister. The meeting would serve as the catalyst for her creation of the plaster bust presented here.

In 1943, Ms. Tribe and her colleagues from the Inspectorate were called upon to assess the interior of No. 10 Downing Street. Prime Minister Churchill was outraged by their unexpected presence and rudely ejected them from the building. Ms. Tribe was so taken aback by the occurrence, she went straight from No. 10 to her studio and sculpted a small bust of Churchill from memory to preserve how he looked that day.

Shortly after the bust was completed, Ms. Tribe donated it as an auction fundraiser item to Mrs. Churchill's Red Cross Aid to Russia Fund. It was graciously

accepted by Mrs. Churchill at Chequers, where Ms. Tribe was given a tour of the house and a letter of thanks.

The plaster bust pictured here is not the one Ms. Tribe donated to Mrs. Churchill. However, it was made from the same mold during the war and signed by Ms. Tribe. Unfortunately, no records can be found which confirm when and how many of these additional copies she produced. The Tribe Churchill busts seldom appear on the market; when they do, they command a price commensurate with their rarity. Thus, the consensus is that Ms. Tribe produced very few. Also, the question remains "why" she made them at all. It's doubtful she produced them for resale but no records show additional donations to Mrs. Churchill's fund or any other wartime charity.

Churchill was referred to as the British Bulldog because of his tenacity. While there are other wartime figurines of cigar chomping bulldogs that bear obvious reference to Churchill, this chalkware piece is the only item which places his head on a bulldog's body.

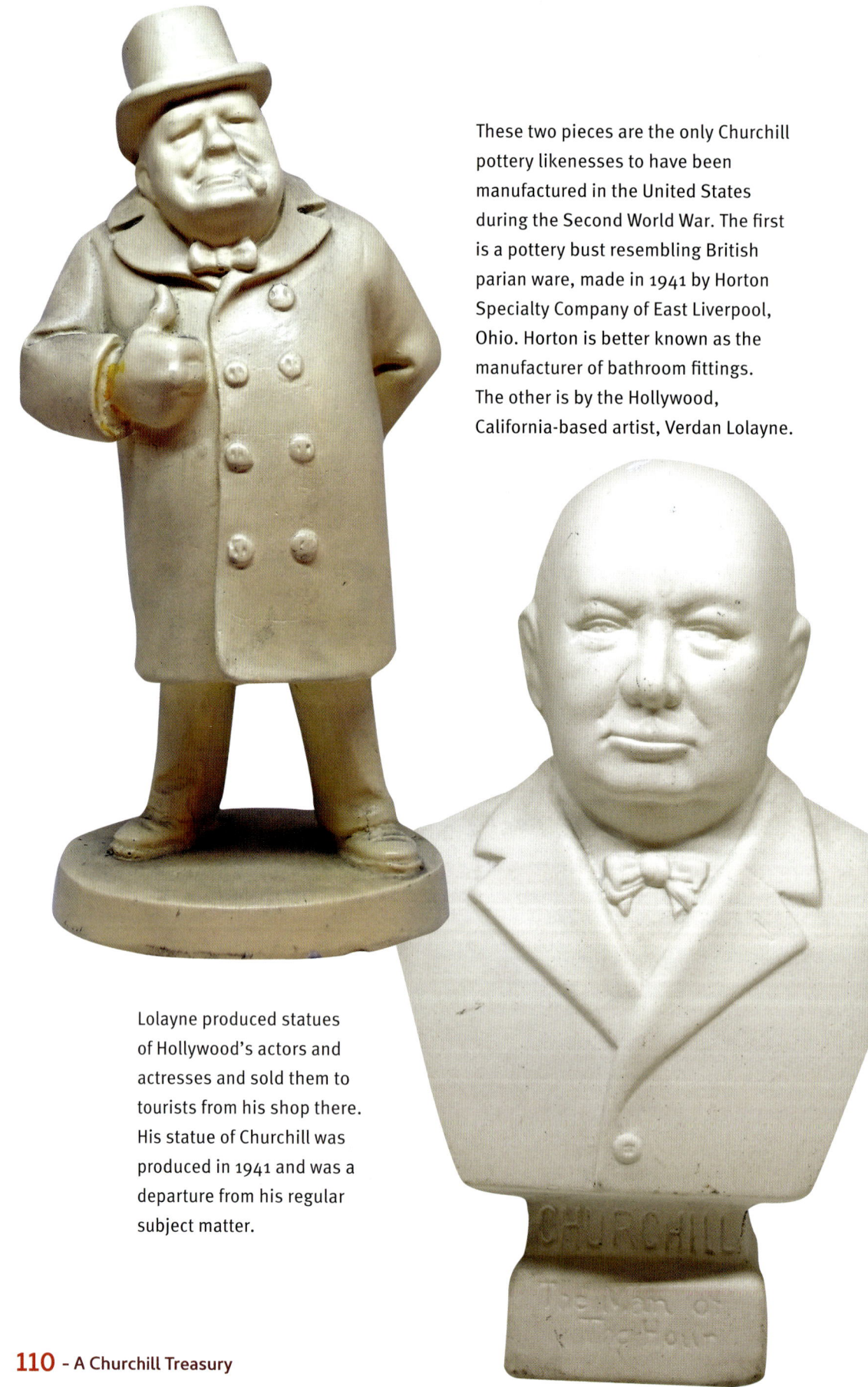

These two pieces are the only Churchill pottery likenesses to have been manufactured in the United States during the Second World War. The first is a pottery bust resembling British parian ware, made in 1941 by Horton Specialty Company of East Liverpool, Ohio. Horton is better known as the manufacturer of bathroom fittings. The other is by the Hollywood, California-based artist, Verdan Lolayne.

Lolayne produced statues of Hollywood's actors and actresses and sold them to tourists from his shop there. His statue of Churchill was produced in 1941 and was a departure from his regular subject matter.

This wartime bust of Churchill was designed and molded by the noted sculptor Peter Lamda for Tallent. It would have sat on the bar in a pub or a counter in a hotel or restaurant to serve as a lighter for cigarettes, cigars or pipes. The back contains a reservoir for lighter fluid. Churchill's cigar pulls out and has a flint on the end to strike against a metal plate in the front of the base. The piece is usually seen in a tan earth tone, but this is the much more rare painted example.

These pieces provide a glimpse into the variety of wartime chalkware and pottery pieces produced in Churchill's likeness. Included are a pottery egg cup, a large chalkware statue of Churchill with an ashtray base and a Churchill figurine pairing with Field Marshal Bernard Montgomery.

World War II – The First Premiership

This signature block, after being pressed onto an ink pad, allowed Prime Minister Churchill's secretaries to apply his signature onto routine letters or other written materials that did not require an in-person signature. This item was acquired from the family of one of the Prime Minister's wartime secretaries.

This colorful puzzle was made shortly after Churchill became Prime Minister in May, 1940. At that time, former Prime Minister Neville Chamberlain was still a cabinet member, Earl Halifax was Foreign Secretary, Mussolini and Italy were in the Axis and Stalin and Russia were still allied with Hitler. Churchill, brandishing his sword, makes clear there will be no appeasement and peace treaty with Germany.

Hitler and Mussolini are all washed up and left hanging out to dry in the hands of the Great Man in this set of three soap bars. This novelty wartime set was made in British Columbia.

On D-Day, 6 June 1944, the RAF air dropped this two-sided flier over occupied France. It reaffirmed Churchill's assurances that France would soon be liberated by allied forces.

On 30 June 1943, Prime Minister Winston Churchill was presented the Freedom of the City of London, which is a high recognition dating back to antiquity. While Churchill's ceremony was held per tradition at Guildhall, it was also held under strict secrecy mandated by wartime conditions. Invited guests were warned not to divulge the time or place of the ceremony. This set of confidential passes belonged to Paul Bossier, the headmaster of Harrow School attended by Churchill in his youth.

These wartime glue front decals would have been dampened and then adhered to glass.

World War II – The First Premiership

Mrs. Foxwell,
Home Farm,
Sherston,
Malmesbury,
Wilts.

PRIME MINISTER.

This letter was sent from Number 10 Downing Street on Churchill's behalf to the mother of a little girl who made a donation to the war effort. It illustrates one of his greatest attributes- his sensitivity to the British people during wartime.

10, Downing Street,
Whitehall.

25th January, 1941.

Dear Madam,

The Prime Minister desires me to thank you for the cheque for 20 dollars which you sent him on behalf of your small daughter, Zia Foxwell, to be used for the war effort of this country.

Mr. Churchill is at once passing it on to the Chancellor of the Exchequer.

Yours truly,

E. M. Watson

Mrs. Foxwell.

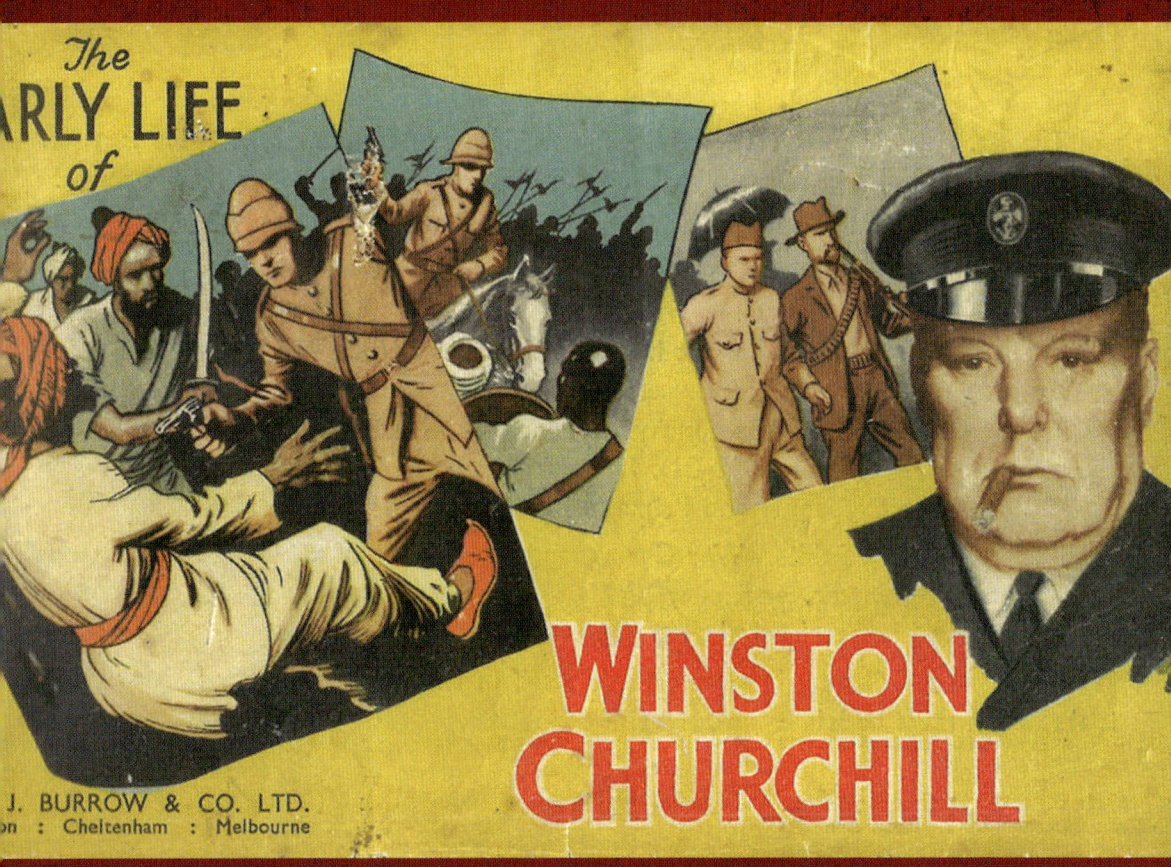

Early in the war, several books for children were published with war-related themes. These were useful tools for parents and teachers when trying to explain the new people, sights, sounds and restrictions the children would experience on the home front. This children's biography of the new Prime Minister was published in 1940, shortly after Churchill formed his government.

Who better than the Prime Minister to push sales of products in wartime? Here, Churchill's image was used on large posters to promote breakfast cereal and beer, as well as on a bookmark to promote a book and stationery store.

On 10 December 1941, the British warships *Prince of Wales* and *Repulse* were sunk by Japanese Imperial Navy bombers in an engagement known as the Battle of Malaya. On this poster, Churchill calls for the increased production of war materials to avenge those losses.

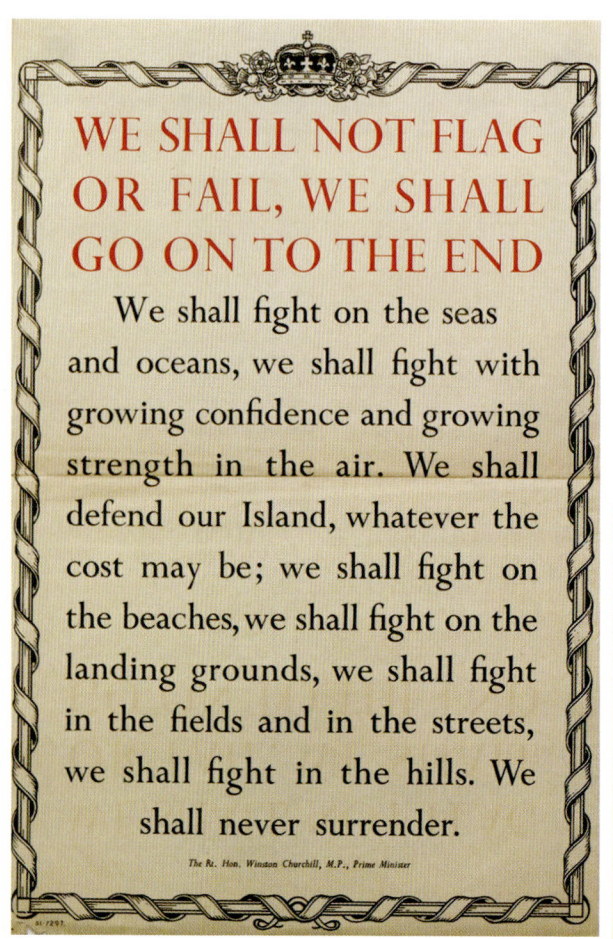

Inspirational excerpts from two of Churchill's speeches were reprinted on these posters in 1941 to bolster citizens' morale. The "Let us to the task" was from a speech given in Manchester on 29 January 1940, while Churchill was still First Lord

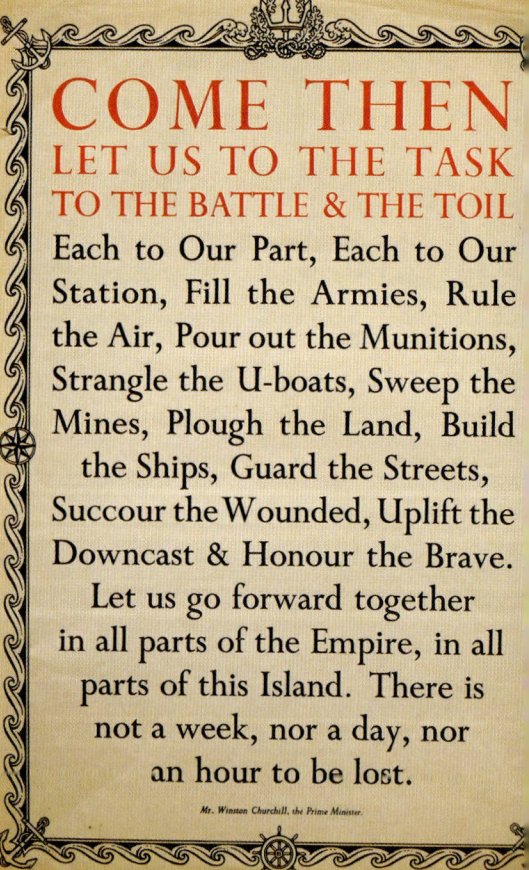

of the Admiralty in the Chamberlain government. The second poster includes excerpts from the "Beaches" speech, delivered before the House of Commons on 4 June 1940, less than a month after Churchill became Prime Minister.

This poster was produced in 1942 and warns that idle chatter could directly impact the war effort. Churchill is the pilot flying the plane (whilst smoking a cigar). As a trained pilot, he would often take the controls of the aircraft transporting him to and from conferences or other important meetings. The photo used in this poster was taken 16 January 1942; Churchill had taken control of the Boeing 314 flying boat transporting him from Washington DC to Bermuda.

The English version of this poster is an iconic symbol of the war. Its message reads "Let Us Go Forward Together." This Hebrew version is significantly rare. Its caption reads "Victory to Victory, Winston Churchill, Premier of Britain." Both posters were printed in 1943. This Hebrew version was used in old Palestine to recruit soldiers for the British Jewish Brigade.

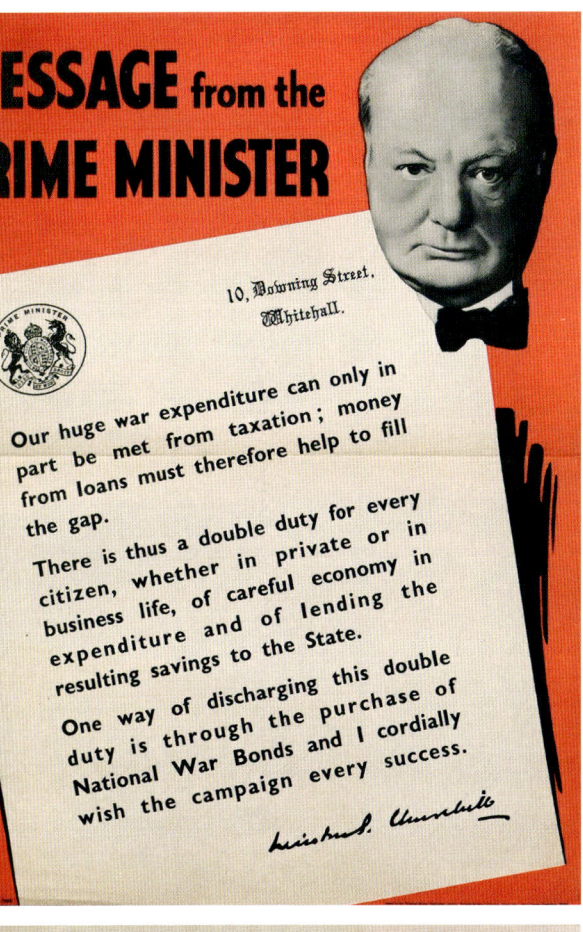

Donating money to fund the war was deemed the responsibility of every citizen who could make a contribution. These three posters employ Churchill's image to encourage adding to the coffers.

World War II – The First Premiership - 125

"... and now, this gentleman is going to tell us how to beat Rommel, save Australia, open a second front Europe, send all our supplies to Russia, wipe out Berlin, strengthen the Army, Navy and Air Force, increa production, double pensions, reduce taxation, avoid inflation, get more coal, settle the India problem, cut o queues, beat U-boats, reorganise railways, stop Nazi bombers, stop profiteering, and have good weather."

Sid Moon was the political cartoonist for the *Sunday Dispatch* from the late 1930s until the paper ceased production in 1961. His original works are highly sought. Here, a poor fellow shivers before the Churchill war cabinet, as he is expected to have solutions to a myriad of problems challenging Britain and the war effort. Given the issues expected to be solved, it appears this cartoon would have been published in October-November 1942.

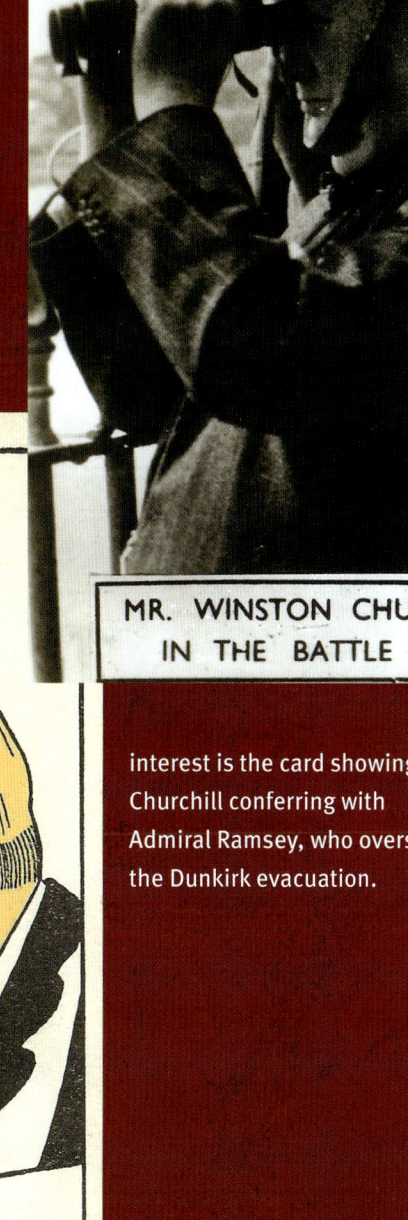

MR. WINSTON CHURCHILL IN THE BATTLE LINE.

The Prime Minister was the subject of many postcards produced during the war. Note the advertising postcard from the Reliable Toy Company where Churchill is the backdrop for a variety of wartime dolls. Also of special interest is the card showing Churchill conferring with Admiral Ramsey, who oversaw the Dunkirk evacuation.

PREMIER CHURCHILL

World War II – The First Premiership

MR. WINSTON CHURCHILL WEARING HIS STEEL HELMET AND THE SMILE OF CONFIDENCE.

MR. WINSTON CHURCHILL SURVEYS PLAN OF CAMPAIGN.

"We shall defend every Village, every Town and every City"...
THE PRIME MINISTER.

WISBOROUGH GREEN.

And so say all of us.

In 1942, the British illustrator, Agnes Richardson, published her "Working for Winnie" postcard series. The cards depict Ms. Richardson's popular illustrated children doing their part for the war effort.

Prime Minister Churchill was the subject of a variety of wartime cartoon postcards, all done in good humour.

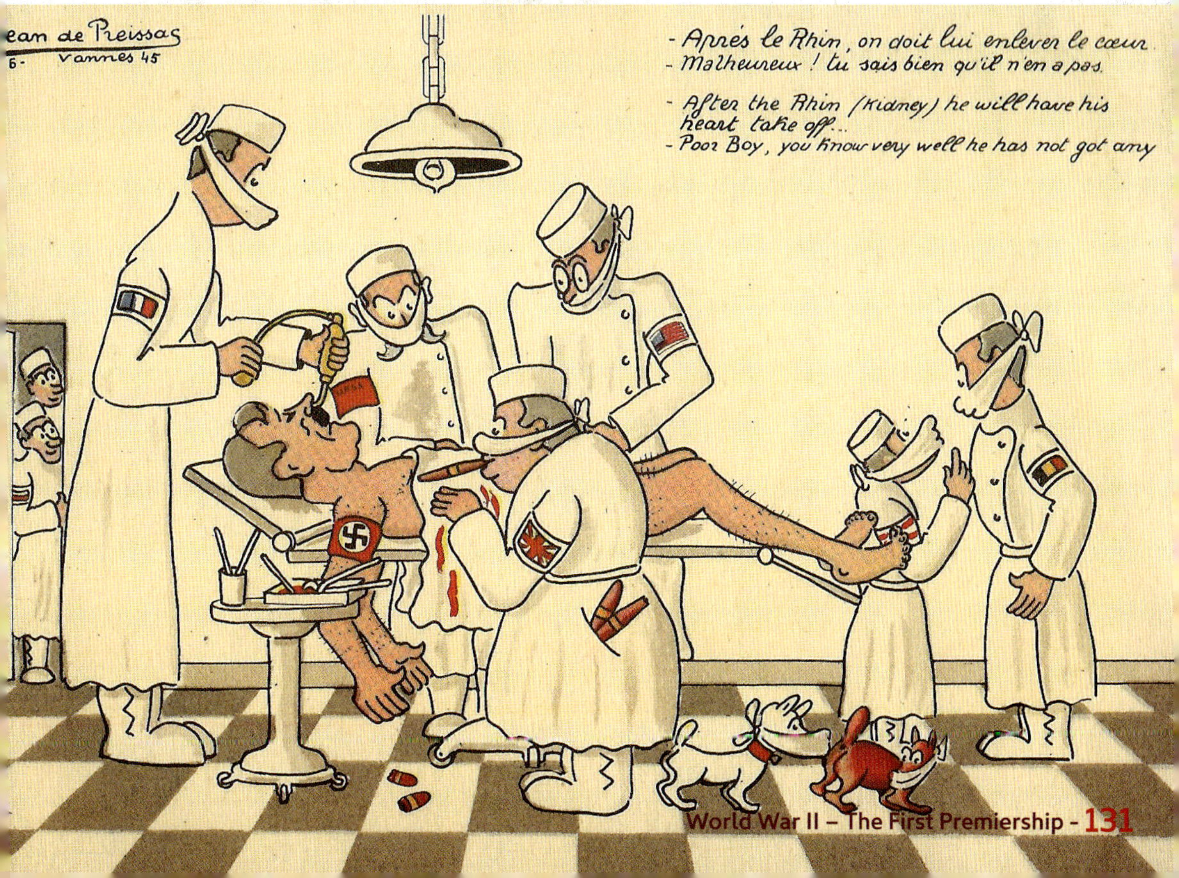

CHURCHILL EN MONTGOMERY AAN HET RIJNFRONT - 4 MRT. '45.

ALL MY OWN WORK BY GRIMES — With acknowledgments To "THE STAR"

"I always listen to dear Mr. Churchill's broadcasts— he always seems to take such an interest in the war."

Churchill was a favorite topic for wartime sheet music. These were intended to be played on a piano, in a pub or at home, with people singing along.

Churchill was featured on various wartime games, meant to be enjoyed by people of all ages. Most of these were handheld games which would not take up valuable space in a blitz shelter. The Jollikin game contains the faces of the allied and axis leaders, each broken into three movable sections. By turning the wheel on the side, the player can create a new person by combining three of the different pieces.

This wall-mounted tobacco cabinet has its inner drawers and pipe rack intact, and features a beautifully carved image of Winston Churchill on the door. The oak cabinet itself is Victorian but a skilled craftsman carved the door during wartime to honor the Prime Minister.

This wartime folk art wooden wall hanging of the Prime Minister was made in Britain's Lake District, where it was discovered and purchased decades later.

World War II – The First Premiership

During the Second World War, Moncton, New Brunswick, Canada was the home of a major Canadian National Railway repair depot and headquarters for the CNR's Maritime division. It was also home to a major supply base for the Canadian Army. This paper knife featuring Prime Minister Churchill was a patriotic souvenir made and sold in the town.

The world's chief cigar aficionado, Prime Minister Churchill, was prominently featured on these wartime wooden cigar boxes, imported from India.

CHURCHILL AND ROOSEVELT MEMORABILIA – PRESERVATION OF THE 'SPECIAL RELATIONSHIP'

Aside from the chapter documenting items from the Atlantic Charter Conference, this chapter is devoted to materials which solely feature Roosevelt and Churchill. Their images appear on some of the best wartime items. At the time, the manufacturers had no way to realize their wares would be preserving one of the most famous political alliances in history. Roosevelt and Churchill met briefly during the Great War and began corresponding with each other when Churchill returned to the Admiralty in 1939. However, after Churchill became prime minister, these two world leaders forged a personal friendship and working relationship which in turn led to what Churchill described as a "special relationship" between the United States and Great Britain. During the war, Roosevelt and Churchill spent 113 days together and exchanged around 2000 messages. Both men came from vastly different political backgrounds; Roosevelt was the elected president of a democracy, while Churchill was the prime minister of a country whose government was a constitutional monarchy. Despite these differences, they were united and driven in their mission to defeat the Axis powers. They forged a bond which defeated an enemy many deemed insurmountable. In doing so, they saved the world.

Please enjoy looking through and studying the items pictured here. They are a fine representative sampling of wartime produced pieces featuring the two prominent allied leaders.

This early wartime felt pennant served to confirm a united cause. Circa 1942.

This unique brown glazed clay water pitcher is the only one known and features President Roosevelt on one side and Prime Minister Churchill on the other. Given its excellent quality and composition, it was most likely made by a skilled and experienced Canadian artisan.

This matched pair of ribbons was made toward the end of the war. While no manufacturer is listed, they are very similar to the British-made Stevengraph ribbons.

This rare and unique pair of maracas was made in Havana during wartime and includes carved images of Roosevelt and Churchill. In December, 1941, Cuba was one of the first Latin American countries to declare war on the Axis. Given its geographical position at the entrance of the Gulf of Mexico and Havana's port, Cuba was an important ally; as a result, it was a direct recipient of Lend Lease and two American airfields were built there to monitor and protect Caribbean sea lanes. Cuba's navy also patrolled the Caribbean and Gulf of Mexico to defend against German U-boats.

This wonderfully graphic poster rightfully proclaims Roosevelt and Churchill as the liberators of the world. Despite a lack of publishing markings, the 'Remember Pearl Harbor" logo is a giveaway this was printed in America.

"Get the Jap", "Set the Rising Sun", and other anti-Japanese sentiments were expressed in America after the surprise attack on Pearl Harbor. On this sheet music cover, Roosevelt and Churchill chase away a Japanese soldier.

Throughout the war, printed calendars featuring images of battles, military leaders or inspirational quotations were popular items sold to promote various charities and benevolent funds. This 1944 calendar features bold images of Churchill and Roosevelt and was sold by ex-servicemen for a veterans' fund.

This large, heavy paper wall mount dates to 1942 and provided wartime inspiration through its quotation and images of Churchill and Roosevelt.

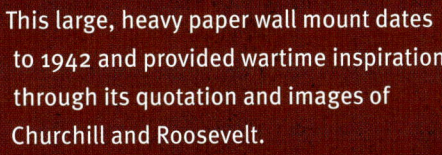

This is a representative sampling of the many wartime postcards featuring Roosevelt and Churchill. Wooden postcards were popular in the 1940's; this one included images of the two Allied leaders.

Many wartime posters or graphics were reduced in size to become large stamps. Often called Cinderellas by collectors, these dressed up a plain envelope with a patriotic message. This beautifully illustrated and detailed piece is actually a stamp!

These wartime glue front paper decals were the forerunners of the modern adhesive-backed bumper stickers. The front glue would be moistened with water, then the decal would adhere to glass. These patriotic examples were made and used in Canada.

Many British porcelain manufacturers produced wartime Churchill and Roosevelt pairings which symbolized their close relationship as allies. Representative pieces include:

- Toby jugs by Minton;
- Busts by Copeland Spode;
- Utilityware ashtrays by Lancasters;
- Charger by Paragon (includes quotations from both);
- Mugs by Paragon;
- Serving dish by Royal Winton;
- Beer schooner by Wade.
- Plate by Wilkinson;
- Busts by Lawton;

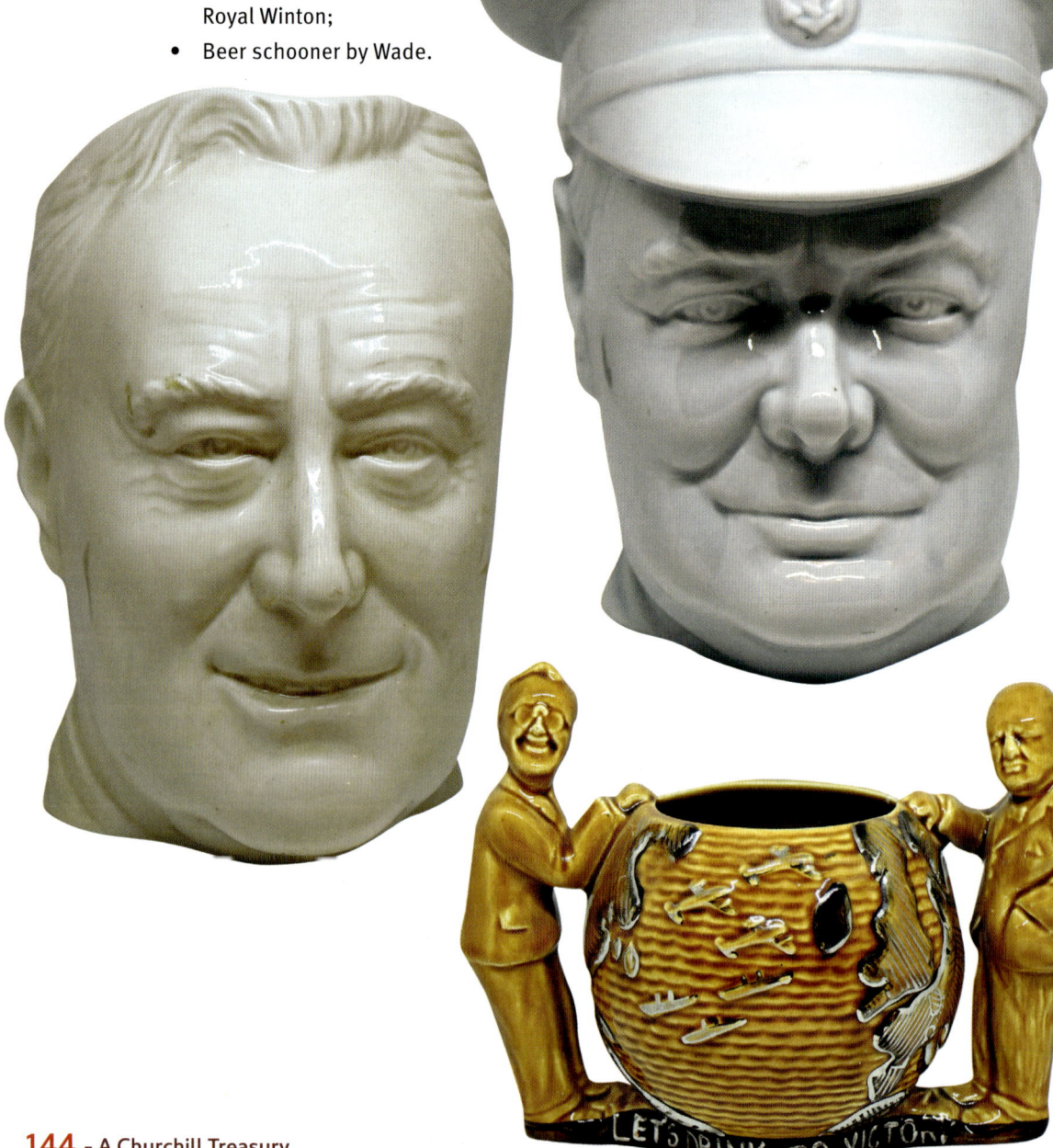

World War II – The First Premiership - 145

World War II – The First Premiership - **147**

BIG THREE ITEMS

While the Big Three signed an anti-Axis alliance pact on New Years Day, 1942, it held most of its meetings from 1943-1945. Items featuring the Big Three – President Roosevelt, Prime Minister Churchill and Marshal Stalin – were manufactured beginning with the 1943 Tehran Conference.

The British maker of this set of Big Three chalkware figurines is unknown, but they are a wonderful addition to a collection. They also come painted in a light tan and mounted on a base or plinth.

This cigarette case is made of Russian silver and features engravings of the Big Three. Notice the Russian spellings of their names.

This American published sheet music shows the Big Three cooking "Axis stew" in a large cauldron. Stalin adds water, Roosevelt spices the pot with a spoonful of ginger and Churchill smiles as he holds up Hitler's head.

French President Charles DeGaulle is included on this nylon kerchief which features the Big Three. Items that include DeGaulle were made in France or Belgium after those countries were liberated in 1944.

This large metal medallion of the Big Three was crafted to be a piece of wall art. Items like this were made from the wreckage of German planes and sold to benefit British wartime benevolent organizations.

The Bovey Pottery began manufacturing its "Our Gang" series of 19 tan glazed figurines in October, 1940. The series included an air raid warden, nurse, pilot and other wartime representatives. It also included the Big Three, with Churchill labeled "The Boss." While all of the Bovey figurines are rare and desirable, Churchill collectors aim for a set of the Big Three.

This wartime beaker is made of Bakelite, an early plastic, and features an attractive image of the Big Three, while titled "United for Victory."

These individually carved figures of the Big Three are spectacular examples of British wartime folk art. Someone with tremendous wood carving skills showed their patriotism by meticulously hand crafting this set, circa 1943.

This set of British-made large oil cloth banners features Churchill, Roosevelt and Stalin. They were designed to hang as a set across the front of a building or on a high wire line across a street. While they were likely made for VE-Day celebrations, they also could have been made earlier as a patriotic street display of wartime support for the Allied leaders.

BATTLE OF BRITAIN COMMEMORATIVES

The Battle of Britain commenced 10 July 1940 and would continue through 31 October. On 20 August, Churchill delivered his iconic "The Few" speech before the House of Commons. Churchill's stirring oratory inspired Great Britain and paid tribute to the brave airmen who would forever be known as "the Few." Items were produced after Churchill's speech that commemorated both the battle and the Few while also memorializing the Prime Minister's eloquent speech. Shown here is a variety of porcelain, a chalkware desk calendar, a nylon kerchief and a wall placard showing a bomber and its crew. Churchill insisted that a bomber crew be pictured to show the Battle of Britain was won by an all-out RAF effort.

In the pre-war and early wartime era, photos could be developed with postcard backings so they could be mailed to friends and family. These are known as real photo postcards (RPPC). This compelling real photo postcard is shown for the first time ever in this book. We do not know the identities of the pictured British couple, but they are very poignant representatives of their time. They've lived through the Battle of Britain and continue to endure the devastation wrought by the Blitz. Despite the hardships and forced changes that have become a part of their daily lives, they are inspired by Churchill's words and courage. They've attached a homemade sign to their carrier to support their Prime Minister and his stirring request for aid from America.

ROOSEVELT, CHURCHILL AND LEND-LEASE

In December 1940, President Roosevelt first proposed Lend-Lease in attempt to provide Great Britain necessary aid by maneuvering around the United States' existing isolationist policies. Under Lend-Lease, the United States would lend, rather than sell, military supplies to Great Britain for use in the war against Germany. Of course, Roosevelt's plan ran into strong opposition amongst the isolationist members of Congress. On 29 December 1940, during one of his iconic "fireside chats," Roosevelt declared "We must be the great arsenal of democracy…"

On 9 February 1941, Churchill broadcast by radio his now famous "Give Us the Tools" speech. Overall, the speech was a report on the progress of the war and aimed at boosting the morale of the British public. The "Give us the tools" comment was actually the last line of the speech, spoken in a crescendo with emphasis as only Churchill could deliver it.

"Give us the tools…" became a popular rallying call amongst the British public. It was printed on a variety of items used to publicly request the necessary assistance Lend-Lease would provide. Examples of those items are included in this chapter. One month later, Congress passed the Lend-Lease Act and Roosevelt signed it into law on 11 March. Roosevelt quickly ordered large quantities of American food and war materials to be shipped to Britain.

The well-established British porcelain manufacturer James Kent produced some wonderful pieces in 1941 to celebrate the passage of Lend-Lease. First, a plate with a raised Florentine border features President Roosevelt and Prime Minister Churchill along with a naval destroyer. Providing Britain with surplus American destroyers was a key component of Lend-Lease and proved vital in defending North Atlantic shipping convoys from German U-boat attacks. Additionally, James Kent produced a series of plates, mugs and other useful daily kitchenware that include images of tanks, bombers and destroyers sent as Lend-Lease aid to Britain by the United States and deemed necessary for defeating the Axis. The backs of each piece include images of crossed British and American flags as a symbol of unity.

Glass slides of current events were often shown in movie theatres prior to the main feature. Here, an image of Big Ben hovers overhead as President and Mrs. Roosevelt and their daughter, Anna, sit at their radio, listening to a broadcast from London. Churchill and Roosevelt began corresponding in 1939 when Churchill returned as First Lord of the Admiralty. Despite the prevalence of isolationism in Congress, President Roosevelt took a keen interest in the progress of the war and pushed for the passage of the Lend-Lease bill.

Given the isolationist laws in America and the isolationist majority in Congress, Lend-Lease was a contentious issue that required President Roosevelt's political finesse for support and eventual passage. Shown here are badges worn by Lend-Lease supporters and opponents.

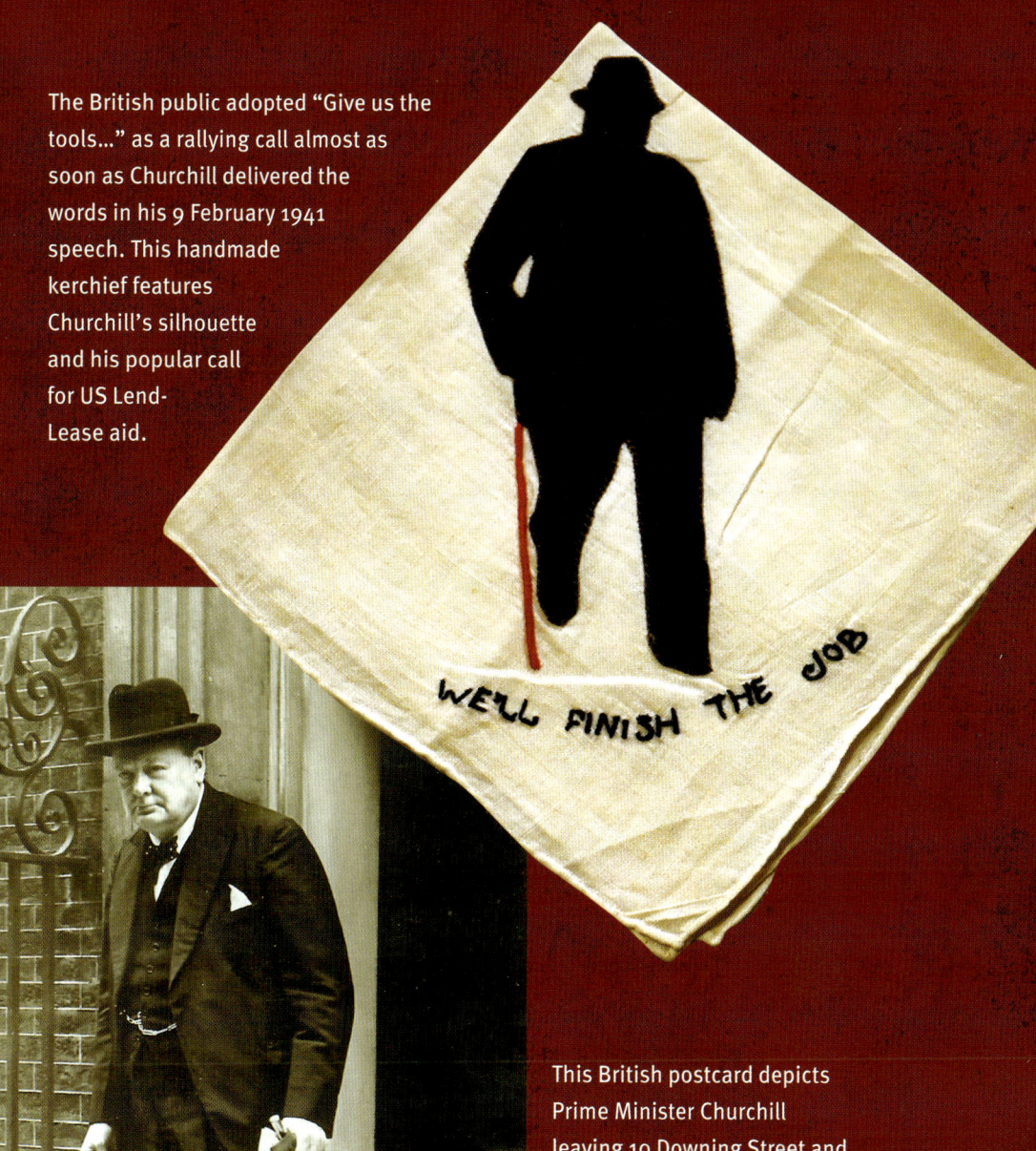

The British public adopted "Give us the tools..." as a rallying call almost as soon as Churchill delivered the words in his 9 February 1941 speech. This handmade kerchief features Churchill's silhouette and his popular call for US Lend-Lease aid.

This British postcard depicts Prime Minister Churchill leaving 10 Downing Street and describes him as a friend in need of US Lend Lease aid. Printed postcards were still a common form of communication in this era and often contained pro-wartime sentiments or images.

World War II – The First Premiership

Traditionally, the newsstands in Britain attracted customers by announcing the latest headlines on large posters printed by the newspaper publishers on cheap paper. The idea was to discard them as the news changed and to replace them with updated headlines. This rare survivor announces the 11 March 1941 passage of Lend-Lease. Imagine the excitement and relief Britons felt when seeing this poster. Help was on the way!

This utilityware beaker was made for everyday use. It features an image of the Prime Minister on the front, and his Lend-Lease rally call on the back.

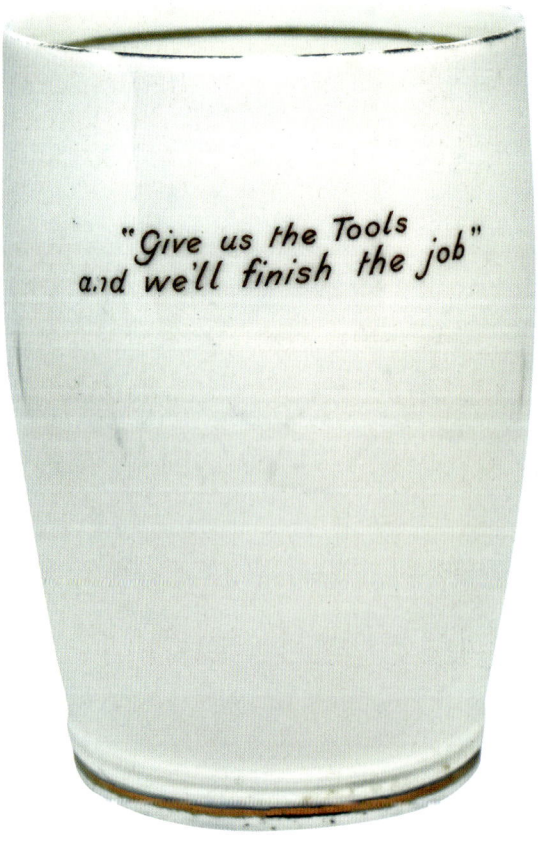

Passage of Lend-Lease was such a big event for Britain, this sheet music was published and sold in England, Australia and New Zealand.

ONE DAY NEARER VICTORY

Churchill to Roosevelt:

"Put your confidence in us. Give us your faith and your blessing, and under Providence all will be well. We shall not fail or falter; we shall not weaken or tire. Neither the sudden shock of battle nor the long drawn trials of vigilance and exertion will wear us down. Give us the tools and we will finish the job."

Roosevelt to Churchill:

The British people need ships.
From America, they will get ships.

They need planes.
From America, they will get planes.

They need food.
From America, they will get food.

They need tanks and guns and ammunition and supplies of all kinds.
From America, they will get tanks and guns and ammunition and supplies of all kinds.

DESIGNED & PRODUCED by THE HARRIS LITHOGRAPHING CO. LIMITED, TORONTO, CANADA

This beautifully graphic placard illustrates the firm resolve of Churchill to continue to fight on and Roosevelt's commitment to provide needed equipment and supplies.

The quotation on this American poster is from Prime Minister Churchill's 15 February 1942 radio broadcast in which he announced the fall of Singapore. Lend-Lease had been in effect since March, 1941 – almost one year, but the Japanese attack on Pearl Harbor which brought America into the war had only occurred two months prior. This poster would have been placed in American factories to motivate workers to keep production moving for America and continued aid to Britain.

World War II – The First Premiership

CHURCHILL'S CHRISTMAS IN WASHINGTON

On 22 December 1941, Prime Minister Winston Churchill arrived in Washington. His entourage included British Ambassador Lord Halifax, Minister of Supply Lord Beaverbrook, and Charles Wilson, Churchill's personal physician. This would be the first of Churchill's five Washington visits made between 1941-1945.

The prime minister initiated this trip to Washington two weeks after the bombing of Pearl Harbor to discuss with President Roosevelt how Britain and the United States could best coordinate wartime strategy. The two world leaders had met only four months earlier in Placentia Bay, Newfoundland for the Atlantic Charter Conference. This visit would last three weeks, extending through Christmas and into the new year. Staying at the White House while in Washington, Churchill utilized the second-floor Rose Suite as office space for the British government; messengers routinely brought documents to and from the British embassy. Likewise, Churchill routinely traveled with wartime maps and regularly referenced or consulted them; this trip to Washington was no exception. He tacked his maps on the walls of the Monroe Room, where First Lady Eleanor Roosevelt held her press conferences.

Churchill celebrated Christmas 1941 with President and Mrs. Roosevelt. On Christmas Eve, he joined FDR at the annual White House Christmas tree lighting, moved from Lafayette Park to the White House's South Portico out of wartime caution. The Prime Minister gave a brief Christmas greeting before a crowd of 15,000 gathered for the lighting.

After attending a Christmas Day church service with President Roosevelt, Churchill spent most of the holiday writing and revising the speech he would deliver the next day to a joint session of Congress. Most of Churchill's 26 December 1941 speech to Congress was an attempt to summarize the course of the war from the standpoint of the British people. His goal was to convince the American public that an affective alliance between the United States and Great Britain could win the war and preserve the peace afterwards. At the end of the speech, as he flashed the V sign, Congress gave him a roaring standing ovation.

```
No. 27
CONGRESS OF THE UNITED STATES
Press Gallery
ADMIT BEARER TO WORK SPACE
ON
DEC 26 1941

By Order—STANDING COMMITTEE OF CORRESPONDENTS
```

Churchill addressed a joint session of Congress on 26 December 1941. This rare press pass allowed a reporter into the press gallery to view and report on this historic moment.

After addressing a joint session of Congress, Prime Minister Churchill returned to the White House. He suffered a minor heart attack while in his suite that evening. Not wanting to alarm him, his doctor told him he was overworked. Churchill pushed forward and traveled by train to Ottawa and addressed the Canadian parliament on December 30. He then returned to Washington to continue his work at the White House.

This badge was worn in Washington DC at the time of Prime Minister Churchill's 26 December 1941 address to a joint session of Congress.

World War II – The First Premiership - 165

ROOSEVELT AND CHURCHILL HOLD PRESS CONFERENCE

Washington, D. C. — President Franklin D. Roosevelt, nearest camera and smoking cigarette in his favorite holder, with British Prime Minister Winston Churchill, smoking a cigar, as they held a joint press conference before the first gathering of the Inter-Allied War Council.

Picturegrams were a popular means of sharing headline news stories in the 1930s-1950s. They were printed posters that would slide into holders in drug stores, restaurants, movie theatres or other public places to allow customers a quick glimpse of current headlines. They would be changed a few times a week and thrown away as the news changed. This surviving Picturegram is dated 29 December 1941 and shows President Roosevelt and Prime Minister Churchill holding a press conference. Churchill would have successfully addressed a joint session of Congress three days earlier and his Washington visit was a very popular news story.

William Sandeson was a noted American editorial cartoonist who began his career in 1937 drawing for the New Orleans Item-Tribune. In 1941, he was employed by the St. Louis Star-Times as editorial cartoonist, art director and picture editor. This original piece of Sandeson's art was created during Prime Minister Churchill's December, 1941 visit to Washington. Churchill brings his blank easel to Washington, ready to paint a word picture describing the mutual benefits of a wartime defense strategy with the United States.

On New Year's Day 1942, Roosevelt and Churchill visited Mount Vernon and placed a wreath on the tomb of George Washington. That night, they gathered at the White House with representatives of several Allied countries to sign a joint declaration to fight the Axis powers together, and that none would negotiate a separate peace. At President Roosevelt's suggestion, this agreement was titled "A Declaration by the United Nations."

Churchill returned to Washington on January 10 after a five-day vacation in Florida. His conferences with President Roosevelt outlined a mutually beneficial strategic framework for defeating the Axis. Roosevelt reaffirmed his belief from the Atlantic Conference that Germany needed to be defeated first. They also agreed to invade North Africa later in 1942, a move that would be the precursor to the Allied landings in Italy and France. At Roosevelt's insistence, Churchill agreed to the concept of supreme allied commanders in Europe and Asia to coordinate the war effort.

Churchill left for England on 14 January 1942. His trip was lauded by the British press, who viewed his discussions with President Roosevelt and their established plans a turning point in the war.

WARTIME CONFERENCES

The wartime conferences were confidential strategy sessions with very little publicity. With the exception of the Atlantic, Tehran and Cairo Conferences, items from these conferences are prohibitively rare and usually consist of passes and other paper items used by those who actually participated.

ATLANTIC CHARTER COMMEMORATIVE ITEMS

From 9 to 12 August 1941, President Roosevelt and Prime Minister Churchill held their Atlantic Charter conference aboard naval ships in Placentia Bay, off the southeast coast of Newfoundland. This was the first time the two leaders met as heads of their respective governments. Conditions included the utmost secrecy with no press coverage to avoid the threat of German U-Boat attacks or criticism by American isolationists. The meeting was not disclosed to the public until 14 August, after the Atlantic Charter was written and signed.

The Atlantic Charter was a declaration of universal freedoms and a call for postwar disarmament. It is considered one of the initial steps toward the establishment in 1945 of the United Nations. Given this was the first wartime meeting of Roosevelt and Churchill, and that it culminated in a joint declaration of human rights, many items were produced shortly afterward to commemorate this historic event. A representative variety is shown here.

This intricately-designed handmade needlepoint was made to commemorate the Atlantic Charter and its declaration of freedoms.

The Atlantic Charter

THE President of THE UNITED STATES OF AMERICA and the Prime Minister, Mr. *Churchill*, representing HIS MAJESTY'S GOVERNMENT IN THE UNITED KINGDOM, being met together, deem it right to make known certain common principles in the national policies of their respective countries on which they base their hopes for a better future for the world.

1. Their countries seek no aggrandizement, territorial or other.

2. They desire to see no territorial changes that do not accord with the freely expressed wishes of the peoples concerned.

3. They respect the right of all peoples to choose the form of government under which they will live; and they wish to see sovereign rights and self-government restored to those who have been forcibly deprived of them.

4. They will endeavor, with due respect for their existing obligations, to further the enjoyment by all States, great or small, victor or vanquished, of access, on equal terms, to the trade and to the raw materials of the world which are needed for their economic prosperity.

5. They desire to bring about the fullest collaboration between all nations in the economic field with the object of securing, for all, improved labor standards, economic advancement and social security.

6. After the final destruction of the Nazi tyranny, they hope to see established a peace which will afford to all nations the means of dwelling in safety within their own boundaries, and which will afford assurance that all the men in all the lands may live out their lives in freedom from fear and want.

7. Such a peace should enable all men to traverse the high seas and oceans without hindrance.

8. They believe that all of the nations of the world, for realistic as well as spiritual reasons, must come to the abandonment of the use of force. Since no future peace can be maintained if land, sea or air armaments continue to be employed by nations which threaten, or may threaten, aggression outside of their frontiers, they believe, pending the establishment of a wider and permanent system of general security, that the disarmament of such nations is essential. They will likewise aid and encourage all other practicable measures which will lighten for peace-loving peoples the crushing burden of armaments.

FRANKLIN D. ROOSEVELT

WINSTON S. CHURCHILL

August 14, 1941

After the 14 August 1941 announcement of the signing of the Atlantic Charter, poster sized copies were printed and distributed throughout Britain and the United States. This declaration of human rights was considered such a pivotal document, efforts were made to ensure its pronouncements were known to all.

This colorful wall placard features Roosevelt and Churchill as partners in promoting the universal freedoms announced within the Atlantic Charter.

Various porcelain and chalkware commemoratives were produced to commemorate the Atlantic Conference. These two have been selected for illustration as among the best and least common. The large, gaudy porcelain flower vase was produced by Falconware. The chalkware shelfware item piece bears no maker's mark but is well executed in the shape of an ocean wave.

World War II – The First Premiership - **171**

Postcards and sheet music were also produced to commemorate the Atlantic Conference. The American military officer accompanying President Roosevelt was his son, James, who assisted the President with his mobility.

1943 QUEBEC CONFERENCE

QUEBEC CONFERENCE 1943
GENERAL PASS
COVERING ALL CONFERENCE PREMISES

The bearer General H. H. Arnold whose signature appears hereon, is permitted to enter ALL premises used for Conference purposes during the progress of the Conference.

S. T. WOOD, Commissioner, Royal Canadian Mounted Police.

PASS NO. 4

Signature of Holder

The first Quebec Conference was held 17-24 August 1943. Codenamed "Quadrant", it was a highly classified strategic planning session, so there were no wartime commemorative items produced. This is the personal pass of General Hap Arnold, signed and carried by him at this conference. Note this is pass number 4; numbers 1-3 would have been distributed to President Roosevelt, Prime Minister Churchill and Canadian Prime Minister MacKenzie King. D-day planning was discussed at this conference and as commanding general of the United States Army Air Forces, General Arnold would have been an integral participant in those planning sessions.

ITEMS COMMEMORATING THE CAIRO AND TEHRAN CONFERENCES

The Cairo conference of allied leaders was held 22 to 27 November 1943 and included President Roosevelt, Prime Minister Churchill and Republic of China leader Chiang Kai-shek. The Conference ended with the completion of the Cairo Declaration, which contained the overall strategic plan to win the war in the Pacific. The Tehran Conference began the following day, attended by Roosevelt, Churchill and Soviet Premiere Joseph Stalin. On 30 November, they completed a preliminary plan codenamed Operation Overlord, which outlined the June, 1944 invasion of Europe. Items were produced to commemorate both of these historic conferences. Since the conferences were held back-to-back, some of the items were manufactured to cover both, rather than one or the other.

This handmade wooden chair and table set features Churchill, Roosevelt and Stalin and is typical of the items made in Egypt as souvenirs of both the Cairo and Tehran conferences.

This large kerchief or scarf was made after the Cairo and Tehran Conferences to include Stalin and Chiang Kai-shek amongst the wartime allied leaders.

In an era where fountain pens were still very much in use, blotters or pen wipes were favored giveaway items used to advertise businesses. These two blotters were made after the Cairo and Tehran Conferences. Not only do they advertise a bank and an insurance company, they also include Stalin and Chiang Kai-shek amongst the wartime allied leaders.

This Italian language poster was printed by the United States War Department at the conclusion of the Tehran Conference to announce and promote the agreement of the United States, Great Britain and the Soviet Union to open a second front to defeat Germany.

World War II – The First Premiership - 177

CASABLANCA CONFERENCE

The Casablanca Conference was attended by President Roosevelt an Prime Minister Churchill and was held 14-24 January 1943. The two principal allied leaders agreed to only accept an unconditional surrender from Germany. This badge was made shortly afterward as a wartime patriotic souvenir.

1944 SECOND QUEBEC CONFERENCE

Codenamed "ANFA", the second Quebec Conference was held 12-16 September 1944. It was a high-level military conference attended by the British and American governments. Topics of discussion included allied occupation zones in a demilitarized Germany and continued Lend Lease aid. Also, plans were developed at this conference to drop the atomic bomb on Japan.

A press pool attended the Second Quebec Conference, but were not allowed into confidential strategy meetings. They received selected briefings after the fact. This press card was used at the conference by American journalist Richard Strout, who was an acclaimed reporter for over fifty years for the *Christian Science Monitor* and the *New Republic*.

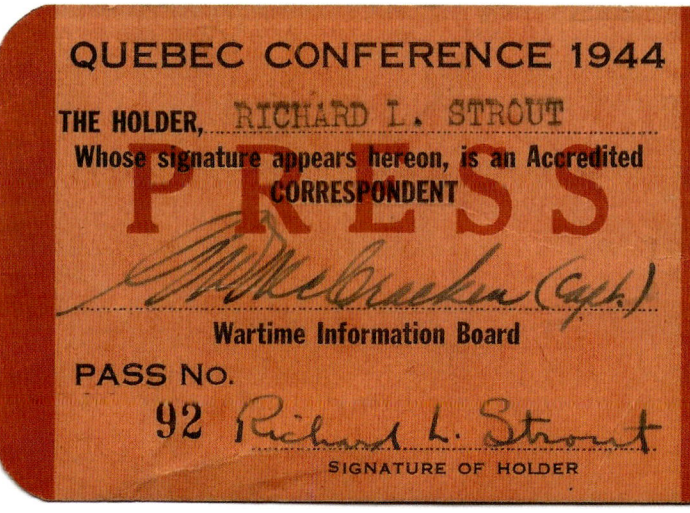

Major General Sir Noel Galway Holmes, Deputy Quartermaster General of the British War Office, attended this conference with Prime Minister Churchill. Shown here are General Holmes' British delegation ID card and his pass, which allowed him to attend high level meetings.

World War II – The First Premiership

YALTA CONFERENCE

The Yalta Conference, codenamed "Argonaut", was held 3-11 February 1945 and was attended by the "Big Three" – Churchill, Roosevelt and Stalin. Confidential discussions concerned the postwar occupation of Germany by allied troops. Germany, and Berlin, itself, were divided into four occupation zones, each separately controlled by the United States, Great Britain, the USSR and France. This phone directory was used by the American delegation during the conference and was given only to members with restricted access. It not only included on-site telephone numbers, but also lodging addresses.

Yalta, U.S.S.R. - February 11, 1945.   Livadia Palace-Site of conference

RESTRICTED

TELEPHONE DIRECTORY

of the
American Delegation at the

ARGONAUT

Conference of the Big Three

JOSEPH STALIN - - FRANKLIN D. ROOSEVELT - - WINSTON CHURCHILL
Union of Soviet   United States of America   Great Britain
Socialist Republics

Conference covered the period February 3, 1945, to February 11, 1945 inclusive. Held to discuss final phases of the war against Germany and to formulate plans for the peace and post-war period. Armistice terms to be given Germany discussed and also the fields of occupation by Allied troops.

Seal of the USSR

Seal of the USA

British Seal

ARMY COMMUNICATIONS SERVICE

RESTRICTED

1945 POTSDAM CONFERENCE

Codenamed "Terminal", and also called the Berlin Conference, the Potsdam Conference was held 17 July–2 August 1945 in the Soviet Occupation zone of divided Germany. The Big Three and their respective delegations met to discuss the joint administration of Germany, which had unconditionally surrendered nine weeks earlier. The leaders also discussed the new post

war world order. Some historians opine that the first tensions of the following Cold War were expressed here. Prime Minister Churchill lead the British delegation but was replaced by Britain's new prime minister, Clement Attlee, following Churchill's defeat in Britain's July 1945 general election. Also, this was President Truman's first conference, following the death of President Roosevelt in April.

This "Terminal" conference pocket map was distributed to the members of the British delegation. The inside fold out shows where members of the delegation- including the prime minister- resided during the conference. Note that the map differentiates the residence of the prime minister from the residence of Clement Attlee, since it was distributed to the delegation prior to Churchill's defeat in the July general election.

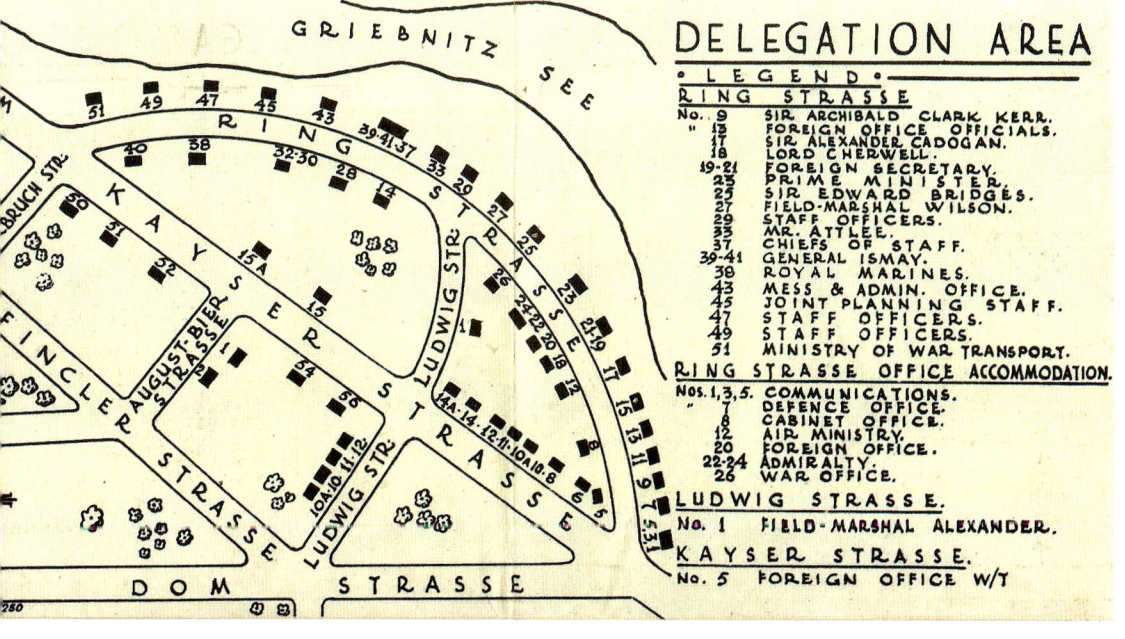

Major General Sir Noel Galway Holmes, Deputy Quartermaster General of the British War Office, accompanied Prime Minister Churchill to Potsdam, and continued as a member of the British delegation when Churchill was replaced by the new prime minister, Clement Attlee. Shown here is General Holmes' conference ID card – note that it is in both English and in Russian. Also shown is General Holmes' card identifying him as a member of the British delegation.

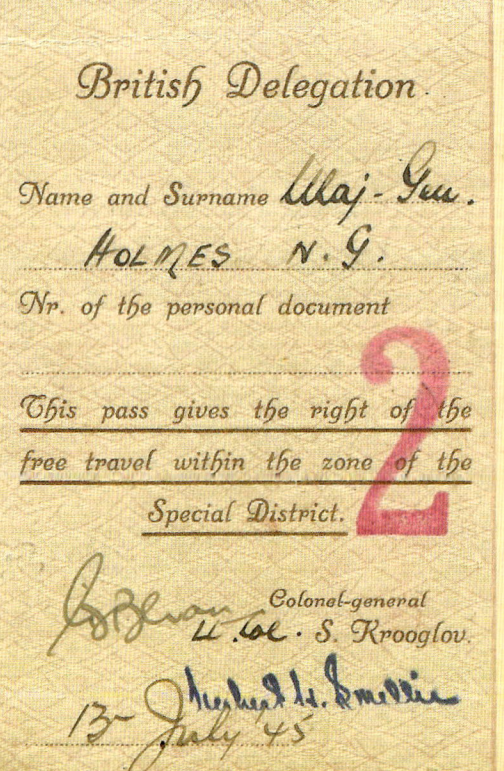

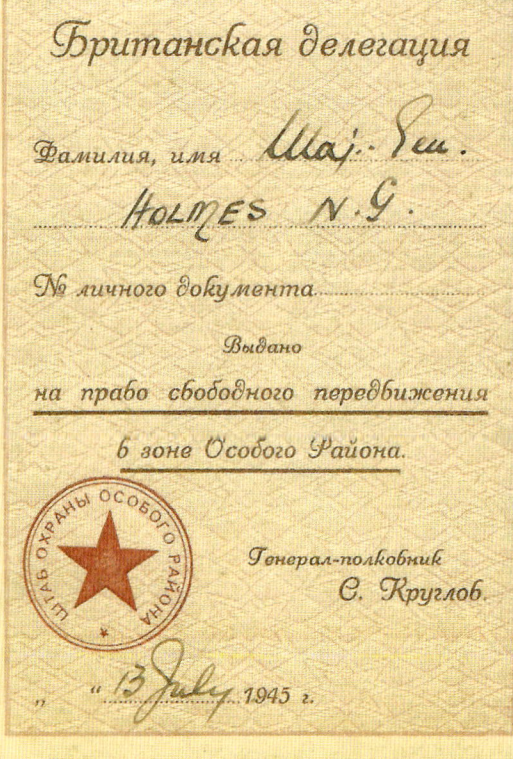

MRS. CHURCHILL'S AID TO RUSSIA FUND.

After Nazi Germany made its 1941 advance into Russian territory, Russia was in dire need of nonmilitary goods to sustain its civilian population. Clementine Churchill, the wife of the Prime Minister, volunteered to chair "Mrs. Churchill's Red Cross Aide to Russia Fund." This organization, under the auspices of the British Red Cross, focused on raising money to supply the Russian people with food, medicine and clothing. King George VI and Queen Elizabeth donated GBP 1000 shortly after the fund was announced, and many citizens donated by having a penny deducted from their weekly pay. By war's end, Mrs. Churchill's fund had raised over GBP 3M to aid Russia's citizens. For her efforts, Russia awarded her the Red Banner of Labour. The posters pictured here were used to promote the fund.

VICTORY THEMED MEMORABILIA

The variety of unique historical pieces included within this section have Victory as their theme. Some were made for VE or VJ Day, while others include the "V for Victory" which is so synonymous with Churchill that it merits special mention.

During a 14 January 1941 BBC European Service broadcast, exiled Belgian politician Victor De Lavaleye proposed the letter V as a rallying emblem for occupied Belgium. De Lavaleye asserted that the V stood for Victoire (Victory) in French and Vrijheid (freedom) in Flemish. He called upon the people of Belgium to publicly write the letter V wherever they could. The V was an immediate success and was chalked or painted on buildings and sidewalks in occupied Belgium, the Netherlands and Northern France.

The BBC soon recognized the success of the V movement and began their own campaign called 'V for Victory'. The campaign was the brainchild of radio presenter Douglas Ritchie who called himself 'Colonel V. Britton' on his broadcasts. He called his listeners the V Army and encouraged them to spread the symbol throughout Europe. Colonel Britton's V campaign was launched during his 18 July 1941 broadcast and included a special message from Prime Minister Winston Churchill; concerning the power and widespread use of the "V" sign.

Similarly, it was soon discovered that the Morse telegraphic code for V was three dots and a dash (. . . —) which were also the opening notes of Beethoven's Fifth Symphony. They were then used as melodic opening theme for Colonel Britton's BBC broadcasts.

Churchill began flashing the V sign so often, that it became his signature. Besides his cigar and Homburg, it's the most recognized and enduring Churchillian symbol. We still flash the V for a variety of occasions, symbolizing Victory as Churchill did himself.

Many scholars consider the V for victory campaign the most successful propaganda campaign in history. During the Second World War, the V was utilized along with Churchill's image on numerous pieces of home front memorabilia, including badges, porcelain, paper items and textiles. Thankfully, many of these pieces have survived and are pictured in this chapter. Unless specifically noted, it is difficult to ascertain whether a V item was made for V-Day or earlier during the war. They are both included in the chapter to illustrate the variety of materials made utilizing the V symbol.

Pocket mirror

Victory hat

Victory poster

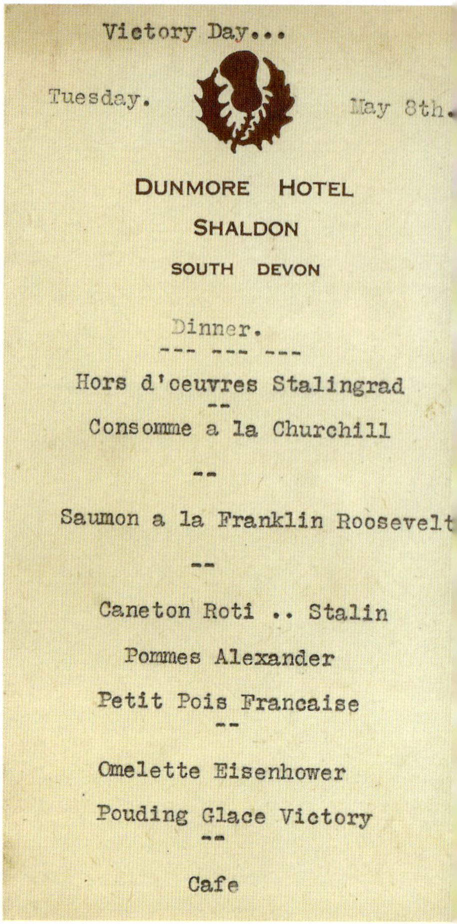

VE Day special restaurant menu

```
Victory Day...
Tuesday.            May 8th.

      DUNMORE  HOTEL
        SHALDON
        SOUTH  DEVON

           Dinner.
        --- --- ---
    Hors d'oeuvres Stalingrad
              --
      Consomme a la Churchill
              --
    Saumon a la Franklin Roosevelt
              --
      Caneton Roti .. Stalin
        Pommes Alexander
       Petit Pois Francaise
              --
       Omelette Eisenhower
       Pouding Glace Victory
              --
              Cafe
```

Paper napkin

Ashtray made from brass battlefield scrap

Batik banner or wall hanging, French Indonesia

Allies Belgian liberation badge

World War II – The First Premiership - **187**

Australian T.B. Appeal badge

Handpainted handkerchief

Spanish tapestry

188 - A Churchill Treasury

Churchill victorious leader badge

WSC Victory glass frame

Russian made rug

V Day bottle opener made of aircraft aluminum

World War II – The First Premiership

Allied leaders wall calendar

Victory celebrations badge

Paper victory pennant

VE Day banner

CHAPTER SIX

1945 Election – 1952 Second Premiership – Death in 1965

The last section of this book covers the last 20 years of Sir Winston's life. It begins with historical pieces relating to the dissolution of the wartime coalition government and ends with his passing away in 1965. While many his age would have chosen to retire, Sir Winston remained active on the world stage and engaged in politics. He would serve as premiere a second time and devote a great deal of time and energy warning of the Cold War dangers posed by the Soviet Union, including dangers posed by nuclear weapons.

A general election was held 5 July 1945 but the results were delayed until 26 July to allow the votes to be sent and counted from the soldiers still serving overseas. At the time, Churchill was attending the Potsdam Conference but flew home to be present for the general election results. The Conservatives expected to win, as Churchill was still tremendously popular; while Prime Minister, his approval rating never fell below 78%. However, the Conservatives suffered a landslide defeat, with Labour winning 393 seats to the Conservatives' 213. Churchill was out, and Labour's Clement Attlee would be his successor. In fact, Attlee took Churchill's place at Potsdam and resumed conference negotiations.

Churchill remained in Parliament as leader of the opposition, and would serve again as prime minister beginning in 1951 when the Conservatives returned as the majority party. From 1945 to 1951 he was quite active, not only as a vocal dissenter and critic in the House of Commons but also in his private life. This period is notable for the publishing of his five-volume war memoirs beginning in 1946. Still a popular and greatly admired world leader, his memoirs were published both in Britain and the United States, one volume annually. The income from the sales of his memoirs would allow Churchill and his family to live comfortably for the remainder of his life.

This period is also remembered for his "Iron Curtain" speech delivered at the invitation of President Harry Truman on 6 March 1946 at Westminster College in Fulton, Missouri. Titled "Sinews of Peace," this speech is considered one of Churchill's finest speeches and one of the best speeches of the postwar era. Through his speech, Churchill warned of the Soviet domination of Eastern Europe and the beginning of the cold war.

Clement Attlee remained prime minister until Churchill's second premiership, which began in 1951. Attlee's government created the National Health Service and National Insurance, which changed Britain's social fabric. When Churchill returned to office after the 1951 General election, he kept Labour's enacted social reforms.

Churchill was 76 years old when he began his second premiership. As he continued to lead Britain as Prime Minister, his health problems escalated. Many were concerned that he had suffered several minor strokes but was ignoring their warnings and effects. King George VI was among those concerned and commented that he planned to ask Churchill to stand down at the first of the year in favor of Anthony Eden. Unfortunately, His Majesty faced his own serious health challenges and died in February, 1952 without discussing the issue with Churchill.

Churchill's chief focus throughout his second premiership was foreign affairs, particularly Anglo-American relations. His primary concern was the use of the hydrogen bomb in a future war and believed the path to continued peace was through a solid, continued relationship between Britain and America. In furtherance of his belief, Churchill officially visited the United States four times from January 1952 to July 1954.

On 23 May 1945, the Conservative-led coalition government Churchill formed on 10 May 1940 was disbanded. At this critical time, and as a way of saying thank-you for dedication and service, Churchill personally commissioned these bronze medallions and presented one to each member of his coalition government. This is the medallion Churchill presented to Lord Henry Page Croft (1st Baron Croft), who served as Under-Secretary of State for War throughout the coalition's existence.

Churchill's health continued to deteriorate but he continued to delay his resignation. One of his main reasons was that his designated successor, Anthony Eden, suffered long-term health issues after a botched abdominal surgery in April 1953. George VI was succeeded by Elizabeth II. Churchill's colleagues thought he might announce his retirement after the Queen's June 1953 Coronation. However, Eden was still quite ill. In response, Churchill increased his own duties by taking over the Foreign Office. Eden's illness kept him incapacitated through the end of 1953 and he continued to suffer permanent injuries for the remainder of his life. On the evening of 23 June 1953, Churchill suffered a serious stroke which left him partially paralyzed on one side. Despite pain and limitations, he presided over a cabinet meeting the next morning hiding any signs of his incapacity. His condition deteriorated throughout the day, and it was thought that he might not survive the weekend. News of his illness was kept from the public and from Parliament; the official word was that he was suffering from exhaustion. He went home to Chartwell to recuperate and it was not until November that he was fully recovered. In the same year, Churchill accepted a knighthood in the Order of the Garter from Queen Elizabeth II. He had initially turned down this high honor after the 1945 general election.

On 16 October 1953, Churchill was formally notified he had been awarded the Nobel Prize for literature. His Nobel citation mentioned his "mastery of historical and biographical description as well as for brilliant oratory in defending exalted human values." It is commonly stated that Churchill received the Literature Prize for his memoir, *The Second World War*. That six-volume work was unfinished at the time, and not considered. Rather, when the award was presented, Churchill's brilliant oratory as well as selected published works, *The River War, Lord Randolph Churchill, The World Crisis, Marlborough, My Early Life, Thoughts and Adventures* and *Great Contemporaries* were specifically mentioned.

On 30 November 1954, Churchill celebrated his 80th birthday. It was a day of celebration and tributes to his remarkable public service, beginning with a midday celebration at Parliament where 2,500 from both Houses, cabinet ministers and former and present officials from both parties gathered for a televised ceremony. As the Churchills arrived in the hall, a drummer beat out the morse code V for Victory. A portrait of Churchill by artist Graham Sutherland, a gift from both Houses, was unveiled. Gifts continued to pour in from around the world, including a cigar shaped floral arrangement from the State of Israel to six pence sent by a young boy. A celebratory dinner was held later that evening.

Aware that he was slowing down both physically and mentally, Churchill retired as prime minister in April 1955 and was succeeded by Eden. After resigning the premiership, Churchill continued to sit as MP for Woodford but never again spoke in the House of Commons. Over time, his attendance in Parliament diminished. Despite a 1959 Conservative general election landslide, Churchill's own majority in Woodford fell by more than a thousand. After that election, Churchill was recognized as the longest serving MP, and the only one serving who had been elected during the reigns of both Queen Victoria and Queen Elizabeth II. As such, he was

The Parliamentary Press Gallery was created in May 1803, wherein part of the Commons public gallery was designated for the press. In modern times, the Gallery includes over 300 participating news agencies. Winston Churchill was the guest of honour at the 23 April 1945 Gallery Luncheon. The front of the event's program depicts History bestowing Churchill with a knight's helmet, while various hat boxes depict the wartime conferences he attended. The back of the card includes the luncheon's toasts list.

named *Father of the House*, the MP with the longest continuous service.

Churchill stood down for Woodford MP before the 1964 general election. He had been dividing his time between Chartwell and his London home at Hyde Park Gate. The Churchills were also frequent travelers to the French Riviera. In 1963, by Act of Congress, President John F. Kennedy proclaimed Churchill an honorary citizen of the United States at a ceremony in Washington. Churchill was too ill to travel to the ceremony, so he sent his son, Randolph, in his place. On 27 July 1964, Churchill was present in the House of Commons for the last time. One day later, at Churchill's Hyde Park Gate home, a deputation headed by Prime Minister Sir Alec Douglas-Home, presented him with a unanimous resolution of gratitude passed by the House of Commons.

Churchill suffered his final stroke on 12 January 1965. He died nearly two weeks later on the 24 January, seventy years to the date of the death of his father, Lord Randolph. On 30 January, Churchill was a given a state funeral, the first for a non-royal person since the 1898 funeral of Prime Minister William Evert Gladstone. He is buried in the Churchill family plot at St. Martin's Church, Bladon, near Blenheim Palace, his ancestral home and place of his birth.

This paper decal features the Big Three and is a surviving souvenir of the 1945 conference which formed the organization known today as the United Nations. Initially, the idea of having a permanent world organization was discussed by representatives of the United States, Great Britain, the Soviet Union and China at a business meeting on 7 October 1944 at Dumbarton Oaks in Washington, DC. Subsequent discussions culminated in a declaration at the Yalta Conference that representatives of the united nations would meet on 25 April in San Francisco, California to integrate the Dumbarton Oaks proposals into a formal charter. The conference convened as planned on 25 April, but without one of its principals, President Franklin Roosevelt. FDR died on 12 April, just a few weeks prior. However, President Harry Truman, his successor, recognized the vital role the United Nations would play in the postwar world and insisted that the conference not be postponed.

there are not enough women...

Shown here are examples of campaign materials used in the 1945 general election.

..who know HOW MUCH THEY OWE TO THE CONSERVATIVES!

1. MR. CHURCHILL'S WAR-TIME GOVERNMENT AND SOCIAL SERVICE

Mr. Churchill led the nation in war while, at the same time, he and his Ministers planned for peace. The social measures now coming into force from higher old age pensions to help-in-homes schemes were the work of the Coalition Government during those war years. Progressive social reform has always been a Conservative ideal.
—the Tories did this

2. FAMILY ALLOWANCES
Winston Churchill's plan

The scheme for Family Allowances was entirely planned, like many other important social reforms, during the war by Mr. Churchill's war-time Government. It was passed into law in June, 1945, by the Conservative Caretaker Government.
—the Tories did this!

3. THE NATION'S FOOD
Fair shares for all

When war came, the Tory Government at once put into operation their plan for equal food distribution—fair shares for all. War-time rationing, the fairest in the world, was entirely planned by the Conservative Government and brilliantly carried out by **Lord Woolton**.
—the Tories did this!

4. NATIONAL HEALTH SCHEME

The first proposals for this far-reaching scheme were brought in by Mr. Churchill's Government in 1944. It is the continuation of many Health Acts developed by Conservative Governments during the last 60 years to cover maternity and child welfare, and health insurance services.
—the Tories did this!

HELP HIM FINISH THE JOB

*We've beaten the Hun,
But there's more to be done.*

- We must defeat Japan.
- We must put Britain back on her feet again.
- We must co-operate with other nations to ensure that a durable peace follows victory.

These are tasks calling for sane and experienced statesmanship.

VOTE CONSERVATIVE
SUPPORT MR. CHURCHILL AND NATIONAL GOVERNMENT

3785   Printed and published by Vacher & Sons Ltd., Westminster, S.W.1

THURSDAY, JULY 5th
VOTE FOR THE CHURCHILL CANDIDATE AND HELP TO FINISH THE JOB.

COUNTRY BEFORE PARTY

Mr. Churchill, March 15th, 1945, said:—

"I shall seek the aid not only of CONSERVATIVES but of men of goodwill of any party, or no party, who are willing to serve, and thus invest our Administration with a national character.

"And if the verdict of the nation should still leave us responsible, that Government after the election will be further re-formed with the sole desire of rallying the strongest forces available to carry our cause to final victory and peace."

- We must defeat Japan.
- We must put Britain back on her feet again.
- We must co-operate with other nations to ensure that a durable peace follows victory.

These are tasks calling for sane and experienced statesmanship.

Who will speak for Britain.

Make certain it is **CHURCHILL CANDIDATES**

ADVANCE BRITANNIA

SHEFFIELD! SEND WINSTON THESE SEVEN—

VOTE NATIONAL

ATTERCLIFFE	BRIGHTSIDE	CENTRAL	ECCLESALL

Group Captain BRIAN PARKER, D.S.O.	Lt. Col. R. BRIAN TAYLOR, O.B.E., T.D. Yorkshire Hussars.	Lt. Col. G. VIVIAN HUNT, O.B.E., T.D. Royal Artillery.	Major PETER G. ROBERTS, Coldstream Guards.

HALLAM	HILLSBOROUGH	PARK
	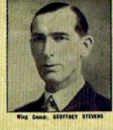	
ROLAND JENNINGS, Durham Light Infantry, 1915-1919.	Lieut. R. H. HOBART, R.N.	Wing Comdr. GEOFFREY STEVENS

ELECTORS OF SHEFFIELD:
VOTE for these men, who will help Churchill to finish the job and worthily represent you at Westminster.

3d.

OUT WITH THE TORIES
By WILLIAM LAUCHLAN

A 12 POINT POLICY FOR THE PEACE

THE CONSERVATIVE PARTY seeks the good of the whole nation, not just one section of it. It stands for:

1. Strong support for Mr. Churchill in waging war against Japan, and in co-operating with America and Russia to keep the peace after final victory.

2. A powerful Britain, able to defend herself and play a worthy part in plans for world security.

3. Vigorous development of the Empire for the benefit of all its peoples.

During his 1945 general election speeches, Churchill often referred to Labour's platform as socialism. In this wonderful original watercolor by an unknown artist, Chef Churchill has cooked the Socialist goose and now serves it up on a platter. Similarly, Churchill's anti-Labour/Socialist message appears on this glass slide which was shown in movie theatres prior to the main feature.

THE SOCIALISTS PLAY FAST & LOOSE
PRAY CHURCHILL COOK THEIR FLESHLESS GOOSE.

CHURCHILL
IS COMING TO SPEAK FOR
CURRAN
WALTHAMSTOW STADIUM NEXT TUESDAY
7.30 p.m.

Printed by GILLETT BROS., LTD. (T.U.), Jewel Road, E.17, and Published by W. J. MARRIOTT, 617 Forest Road, E.17

This poster is a rare survivor of one of the most tumultuous campaign events of the 1945 general election. Churchill came to Walthamstow Stadium on 3 July 1945 to speak on behalf of Charles Curran, a Conservative party stalwart and the candidate standing for MP for Walthamstow West. As Churchill began speaking, he was booed intermittently by the many Labour supporters who had entered the stadium with the intent to be disruptive. At one point, Churchill stopped his speech and told them to "have a good boo." He also began referring to Labour as the "boo party," and "socialist woolgatherers." Walthamstow West was won by Labour in the 1945 general election sweep. Curran only received 17 percent of the vote.

In the 1945 general election, citizens rejected the Conservative Party, not Churchill himself. As Prime Minister in 1945, he still enjoyed 78% popularity. In this rare poster, Wing Commander Roland Robinson identified himself as "Churchill's Man!" rather than as a Conservative Party candidate. During the Second World War, Wing Commander Robinson was the RAF's liaison with the famous Eagle Squadron. He was first elected as MP for Widnes in 1931, a seat he held until 1935. He was then elected MP for Blackpool. His constituency was divided in the 1945 general election. He stood for and was elected MP for Blackpool South and held that seat until his retirement in 1964. He then served as Governor of Bermuda until 1972.

This very special piece of Churchillian history provides an amazing first-person, eyewitness account of an event dramatized in the 2008 HBO movie, *Into the Storm*, starring Brendan Gleeson as Winston Churchill. On the evening of Thursday, 2 August 1945, the original owner of this theatre program and ticket attended Noel Coward's production of *Private Lives*, a three-act comedy starring Peggy Simpson and John Clements at London's Apollo Theatre. This patron not only made handwritten notes about the play and its actors, but also recorded witnessing a very special guest and the ovation he received:

> Notable because Mr. and Mrs. Winston Churchill and daughter sat several rows in front of me. Look just like their pictures. Got a tremendous ovation and he gave the V sign in acknowledgement even as an Ex-Premiere. In a curtain speech, John Clements said "On the night of 2 August 1945, I will always remember that I had the honour of playing before the greatest Englishman (W. Churchill) of our time" and I think he is correct!

Private Lives has been described as one of Mr. Coward's most successful plays and is still performed today.

H. M. TENNENT LTD. and JOHN C. WILSON

present

PRIVATE LIVES

About 2 divorced people who who married others and then with each other on their wedding nite Sophisticated or what have you?!

A Comedy in Three Acts

by

NOEL COWARD

Not liked in Brooklyn

Cast in order of their appearance:

Sybil Chase	PEGGY SIMPSON
Elyot (her Husband)	JOHN CLEMENTS — *star*
	(appeared in the movie — "Mrs. Miniver" plays an excellent piano too)
Victor Prynne	PATRICK BARR
Amanda (his Wife)	KAY HAMMOND — *star*
	An expert in sophistication
Louise	YVONNE ANDRE

Produced by JOHN CLEMENTS

Decor by G. E. CALTHROP

In a curtain speech John Clements said, "On the nite of 2 Aug '45 I will always remember that I had the honour of praying before the greatest Englishman (W. Churchill) of our time."

ACT I. Adjoining balconies of a hotel in France one Summer evening a few years ago.

ACT II. Amanda's flat in Paris some days later. Evening.

ACT III. The same. Next morning.

Scenery painted by Alick Johnstone. Built by Brunskill & Loveday Ltd. The play furnished by the Old Times Furnishing Co., 125 Victoria Street, S.W.1. Miss Kay Hammond's suit and hat in act 3 by Lorian, 38 South Audley St., W.1. Miss Kay Hammond's shoes by Delman, Bond Street, W.1. Miss Peggy Simpson's dresses by Bianca Mosca, at Jacqmar, 16 Grosvenor Street, W.1 Stockings by Kayser-Bondor. Properties by Robinson Bros. Sound Apparatus by Bishop Sound and Electrical Co. Ltd. Cigarettes by Abdulla.

General Manager	For		ELSIE BEYER
Manager and Stage Director	H. M. TENNENT LTD.		VICTOR WESTON
Stage Manager	and		MARJORIE MARKHAM
Press Representative	JOHN C. WILSON		RICHARD CLOWES

Manager	For APOLLO THEATRE	HUGH BAKER

BOX OFFICE (W. SPORREY) Open daily from 10 a.m. to 7 p.m. GERrard 2663

The Management reserve the right to refuse admission, also to make any alteration in the cast which may be rendered necessary by illness or other unavoidable causes.

Ladies are earnestly requested to remove Hats or any kind of Head-dress. This rule is framed for the benefit of the audience, and the Management trusts that it will appeal to everybody, and that ladies will kindly assist in having it carried out.

In accordance with the requirements of the Lord Chamberlain—1.—The public may leave at the end of the performance by all exit doors and such doors must at that time be open. 2.—All gangways, passages and staircases must be kept entirely free from chairs or any other obstructions. 3.—Persons shall not in any circumstances be permitted to stand or sit in any of the gangways intersecting the seating, or to sit in any of the other gangways. If standing be permitted in the gangways at the sides and rear of this seating, it shall be strictly limited to the number indicated in the notices exhibited in those positions. 4.—The safety curtain   lowered and raised in the presence of each audience.

and — I think he is correct!

No longer Prime Minister but still greatly respected throughout the world, Churchill continued traveling to the United States, France and other destinations for relaxing holidays, to enjoy painting and to present speeches. This heavy paper tag was used to identify Churchill's luggage when he traveled.

1945 Election – 1952 Second Premiership – Death in 1965

In 1946, with the urging of President Truman, Churchill was invited by Westminster College in Fulton, Missouri to deliver the annual John Findley Green lecture. Given Labour's landslide victory in the July 1945 general election, Churchill was no longer prime minister, but was leader of the opposition. He was still very popular, even though his party was not.

On 5 March 1946, Churchill delivered his speech at Westminster College, after being introduced by President Truman. The speech is formally known as "Sinews of Peace," but is also known for one of its most famous phrases, the "Iron Curtain" speech. Churchill described the new cold war, and further related that a Soviet "iron curtain" now separated eastern Europe. This speech is considered by historians to be one of Churchill's best, and one of the most pivotal speeches of post-Second World War.

Various items were produced to mark the significance of the day. Shown here are a ticket to Churchill's speech, a campus pass, the official program, pennants, and a button. The larger blue pennant was one of three different colors; blue, yellow and green, used to mark seating in the Westminster campus gymnasium where Churchill spoke.

WESTMINSTER COLLEGE

The John Findley Green Lecture

BY

THE RT. HON. WINSTON CHURCHILL

INTRODUCTION BY

THE HON. HARRY S. TRUMAN

President of the United States

Fulton, Missouri
The College Gymnasium and Swope Chapel
Tuesday, March 5, 1946

Program

Processional, "How Firm a Foundation"

Audience, "Star Spangled Banner" and "God Save the King"

Invocation
    REV. WILLIAM B. LAMPE, D.D.
    Moderator of the Presbyterian Church, U.S.A.

The John Findley Green Foundation
    FRANC LEWIS McCLUER, Ph.D.
    President of the College

Presentation of the President

Presentation of Mr. Churchill
    THE PRESIDENT OF THE UNITED STATES

The Green Lecture, "World Peace"
    MR. CHURCHILL

Conferring of Honorary Degrees by PRESIDENT McCLUER—
    Citation of Mr. Truman, MR. NEAL S. WOOD
    Citation of Mr. Churchill, MR. JOHN RAEBURN GREEN

Solo, "Recessional"   Kip
    MR. JOHN A. FREDRICK

Benediction
    REV. J. LAYTON MAUZE, D.D.
    Pastor of the Central Presbyterian Church, Kansas City, Missouri

Recessional, "Love Divine, All Love Excelling"

WELCOME TO FULTON

CHURCHILL DAY
PARKING INSTRUCTIONS

1. STAY IN LINE—DON'T ATTEMPT TO PARK UNTIL YOU ARE ASSIGNED YOUR PARKING SPACE BY THE PATROL.
2. Follow direction arrows and officer's instructions at all times.
3. You will be assigned to the next available free parking space.
4. The Missouri Highway Patrol is in charge of all traffic and parking.
5. All parking is free—pay no parking fee.
6. Cooperate to make room for all.

TAKE IT EASY—DRIVE SAFELY

Official Souvenir Map and Program
Churchill Day
FULTON, MISSOURI

March 5, 1946

Winston Churchill

Compliments
AUTOMOBILE CLUB OF MISSOURI

Admit **Mr. or Mrs. Fred P. Holt** To Gymnasium
(non-transferable)

Westminster College
John Findley Green Foundation Lecture
delivered by
The Hon. Winston Churchill
introduced by
President Harry S. Truman

Reserved Seat — Section B

Fulton, Missouri   March 5, 1946
Campus opens 1:15 p.m.   Doors close 2:45 p.m.

No. 1104

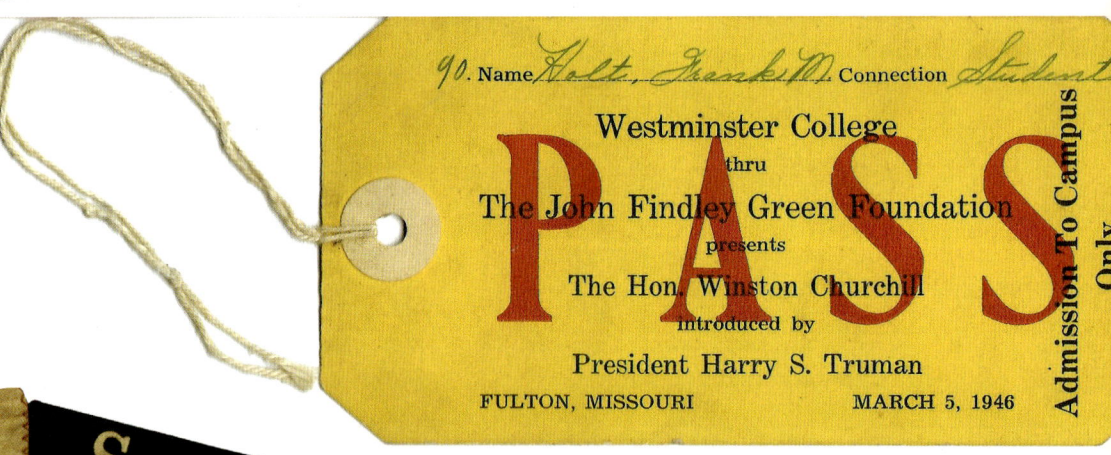

On 7 May 1946, exactly one year after the unconditional surrender of Germany, Winston Churchill was presented with the Freedom of the City of Westminster in a formal ceremony. On 28 March 1947, noted British artist Richard Eurich, RA, completed a large oil on canvas of Churchill's Freedom ceremony, which is displayed in the Westminster Town Hall. The oil on canvas pictured here is one of the last studies completed by Mr. Eurich prior to executing the finished work. This study differs very little from Mr. Eurich's final rendition, with the noted exception that an audience was added to the foreground.

The flier, program and admission badge shown here are artifacts remaining from the 1948 Luton Gymkhana and Churchill's speech there. A gymkhana is a British term which originated in India, meaning a meet featuring a series of competitive athletic, horseback or driving skills. On 28 June 1948, Churchill was the guest of honor and featured speaker at the gymkhana at Luton Hoo, sponsored by Eastern Area of the Conservative and Unionist Association. The crowd totaled around 100,000 and was the largest Churchill had ever addressed in his career. Special trains brought people from all over England to Luton, and a shuttle bus service brought them from the rail station to the gymkhana. Churchill was met with tremendous applause. His speech warned of the encroachment of the Soviet Union in Eastern Europe and that there should be no yielding to dictators.

Winston Churchill began writing his war memoirs shortly after returning home from delivering his 5 March 1946 "Iron Curtain" speech at Westminster College. A team of researchers would gather all relevant documents and Churchill would then draft the text linking them together. As was his practice when drafting his wartime speeches, he preferred dictating his drafts late at night with his secretaries making his corrections and edits until achieving the final product. *The Second World War* was thus published in six volumes between 1948 and 1954, with a combined first printing of over 800,000 copies. This 1948 newsstand advertisement announced that excerpts from Churchill's first volume would appear in the New York Times as a preview for eager readers and potential purchasers.

On 9 October 1948, before an audience of 2,500, Churchill delivered the keynote address for the 69th annual Conservative Party Conference, held at Llandudno, Wales. His speech, titled "Perils Abroad and at Home," warned that world peace would be jeopardized if the Soviet Union ever possessed a greater nuclear capability than the United States, Britain and their allies. This ticket would have allowed the bearer onto the ground floor level of the rostrum area.

This original sketch was drawn by Sir Hugh Dalton, who served as Chancellor of the Exchequer in the Attlee government. It features the two most prominent politicians in postwar Britain, Winston Churchill and Clement Attlee. The sketch was made during an undated Attlee cabinet meeting and given by Sir Hugh to Sir George Mallaby, a cabinet undersecretary on British foreign and defence policy. The sketch was passed down through the Mallaby family as a keepsake of Sir George's public service.

Violet Bonham Carter was the daughter of Prime Minister H.H. Asquith. While living at 10 Downing Street during her father's premiership (1908-1916), she was introduced to many of the instrumental politicians of the Liberal Party, including a young Winston Churchill. The two formed a friendship that lasted around 60 years. In 1965, Lady Violet published *Winston Churchill: An Intimate Portrait*, her recollections of Churchill for the period 1906-1916. In the 1945 election, Lady Violet stood for election as MP for Wells but came in third. In 1951, she stood for MP from Colne Valley. Churchill persuaded the Conservatives to not run a candidate for the seat. As this ticket shows, Churchill also publicly endorsed Lady Violet's candidacy, speaking on her behalf at a meeting sponsored by the Colne Valley Division Liberal Association. Despite Churchill's assistance, Lady Violet lost this election to the Labour Candidate.

Colne Valley Division Liberal Association.

CANDIDATURE OF
THE LADY VIOLET BONHAM CARTER

MEETING

in the **HUDDERSFIELD TOWN HALL**,
Monday, Oct. 15th, 1951, at 7-30 p.m.

To be addressed by The Rt. Hon.
WINSTON S. CHURCHILL,
O.M., C.H., F.R.S.

ORCHESTRA   -   -   2s. 6d.

Published by E. Thorn and printed by Taylor & Clifton, Uppermill

GENERAL ELECTION 1950

WOODFORD PARLIAMENTARY DIVISION
(Comprising Chigwell Urban District and the Borough of Wanstead & Woodford)

PHOTO BY VIVIENNE, LONDON.

The Rt. Hon.
WINSTON S. CHURCHILL, O.M., C.H.

ELECTION ADDRESS

This leaflet was distributed by Churchill during the 1950 general election as he stood for re-election as MP for Woodford. The 1950 general election was held 23 February and was the first in Britain since Labour's 1945 landslide victory. Attlee's Labour government had served a full term. Labour's majority shrank significantly, from 146 to 5. This was also the first general election to be televised, although unfortunately the footage was not recorded.

The 1951 general election was held 25 October, just 20 months after Labour had retained a slim five-seat majority in the 1950 general election. Labour called the 1951 election hoping to increase its majority but just the opposite occurred; the party lost 20 seats while the Conservatives increased their hold by 23 seats. As a result, the Conservatives now had a majority with 321 seats to Labour's 295 seats. With the Conservatives now again the majority party, this election marked the return of Churchill as prime minister. He would serve until stepping down in 1955. Labour would serve as the opposition party for the next thirteen years.

This postcard and booklet are items used in the 1951 general election.

A bit of dry humour...

Although Churchill would need to be chosen by his party to be Prime Minister, public sentiment, as shown by this rare badge, was certainly a factor in their decision.

On 30 November 1951, the Uxbridge Conservative Association celebrated Prime Minister Churchill's 77th birthday by hosting a fundraiser dinner dance. Churchill is prominently featured on the front cover of the evening's program.

British Paramount News was a subsidiary of the American Paramount from 1931-1957 and provided sound reels of news shown in movie theatres prior to the main features. This poster would have been displayed in a changeable frame in the theatre lobby to give patrons a snippet of the daily news and what they could expect to see on the sound reel. This rare survivor was displayed at the very beginning of the second premiership as Churchill entered office.

This ticket admitted the bearer to Churchill's third address to a joint session of Congress. The first two addresses occurred during the Second World War. In this post-war address, he spoke on the need to re-arm Western Europe in the face of a Soviet threat. He also provided reassurance that the "special relationship" was very much intact despite some disagreements regarding strategic interests in the war in Korea and Far East relationships generally.

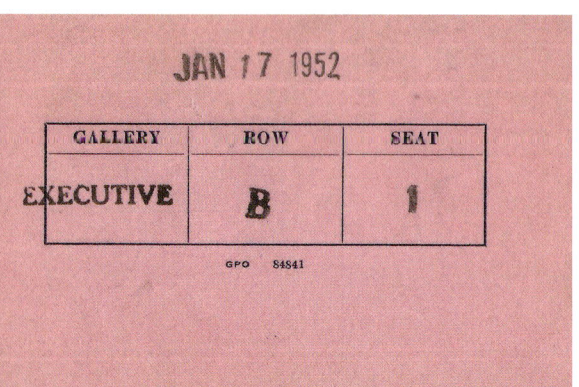

A variety of these chalkware Churchill figurines were made during the second premiership. They adorned shelves and mantles to celebrate Churchill's return. They can be found in many sizes and paint schemes.

1945 Election – 1952 Second Premiership – Death in 1965

Churchill continued to be a popular subject for Toby jug makers and porcelain manufacturers into his second premiership. Shown here are four fine examples. The two Toby jugs were made by Arthur Bowker, Fenton (L) and Kelsboro (R). The nicely detailed porcelain bust has no maker's marks.
The caricature ashtray is actually Swiss.

This unique giant novelty pencil was made during the second premiership as a giveaway promotional item for F. Chambers & Company, Ltd. of Nottingham. It features a wartime portrait of Churchill and an excerpt from his famous wartime "Beaches" speech. Chambers began business in 1915 as a pencil manufacturer and is still in business today.

Shown here are two Churchill metal items- a paperweight and a wall hanger, made during the second premiership.

1945 Election – 1952 Second Premiership – Death in 1965

"One man in his time plays many parts"—with congratulations to Sir Winston Churchill, who tomorrow enters his 80th year

Reprinted from The Sunday Times · November 29 · 19..

On 30 November 1954, Prime Minister Churchill celebrated his 80th birthday, which coincided with the opening of Parliament. The ceremonies began at mid-day with 2,500 in attendance, as speeches and gifts were given from both Houses of Parliament in Westminster Hall. A portrait of Churchill, commissioned by the House of Commons, was unveiled. The painting was later quietly destroyed since the Churchills thought it was very poor likeness . Tributes and birthday gifts poured in all day, including a flower arrangement in the shape of a cigar from Israel and 6 pence from a young boy in Hereford.

The day before his special birthday, the *Sunday Times* published an editorial illustration which was also available for purchase as the poster shown here. It depicts Churchill in the numerous positions and roles in which he'd served his country, with History bestowing a laurel wreath as a birthday honour.

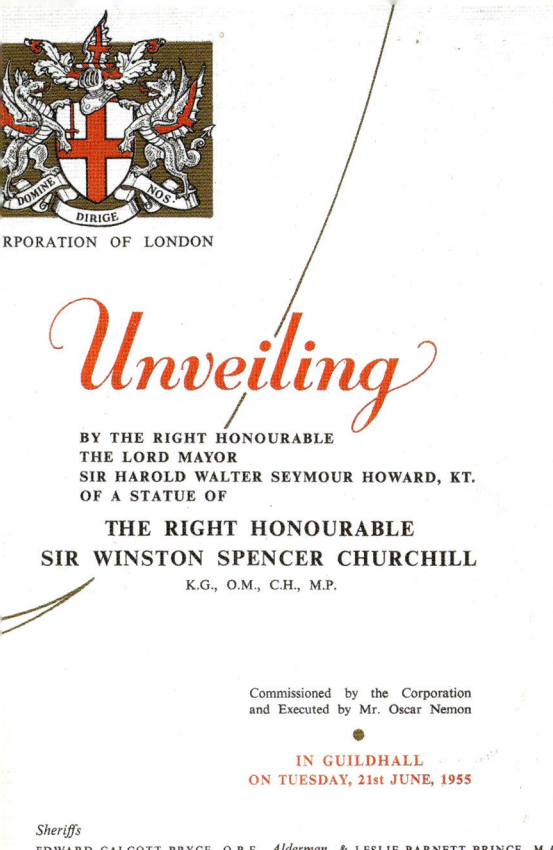

This program is from the 21 June 1955 unveiling of the magnificent seated bronze sculpture of Churchill by Oscar Nemon, in London's Guildhall. Churchill and Nemon first met in Marrakech in 1951; Nemon sculpted a bust of Churchill that Mrs. Churchill thought was an excellent likeness. In 1952, Nemon was commissioned by Her Majesty Queen Elizabeth II to sculpt a bust of Churchill for display at Windsor Castle. Later, in 1970, Nemon's standing bronze statue of Churchill was unveiled at the entrance to the House of Commons in Westminster Palace.

This lovely pair of bookends was crafted in 1955 by the noted British sculptor, Jon Douglas, to commemorate Churchill's second premiership. Note that each bookend includes a different pose of Churchill.

1945 Election – 1952 Second Premiership – Death in 1965

Churchill began painting as a hobby in June, 1915 while on a family holiday. He discovered that painting served to remedy bouts of depression. He started with water colors but eventually transitioned to oils. When Churchill was on active military service in 1915-1916, he even took his painting materials to the Western Front, completing scenes of the landscape and town where he commanded the 6th Battalion, Royal Scots Fusiliers. The Second World War was a different story; Churchill completed only one painting while Prime Minister and gifted it to President Roosevelt. Churchill continued painting into his golden years and completed over 500 works.

One of Churchill's favorite places to visit – and to paint – was the French villa of his long time friend and political ally, Lord Beaverbrook. Lord Beaverbrook's villa was named La Capponcina and located in Cap d'Ail in the South of France. Through almost 50 years of friendship, the Churchills were frequent visitors and even celebrated their golden wedding anniversary there. Churchill first met Beaverbrook in 1911; the young Canadian millionaire had only moved to England the year before, but was already involved in Tory politics. He quickly became a newspaper mogul. During the Second World War, Lord Beaverbrook served as Minister of Aircraft Production, then Minister of Supply and later Minister for Production.

The two original unpublished photos shown here were taken by Lord Beaverbrook's private secretary and acquired from her heirs. They record a visit by the Churchills in September, 1958. Churchill is seated on the terrace at La Capponcina, with an oil painting in progress on his easel. An examination of these photos has determined that Churchill was painting *Monte Carlo from Cap d'Ail*. This finished work currently resides in Churchill's studio at Chartwell.

This palette knife was an 80th birthday gift to Sir Winston Churchill. The tortoise shell handle includes a silver plate upon which his name and birth date are engraved. This piece shows signs of use, where the blade was used to apply oil paint to a canvas. This is one infrequent time when a collector prefers an item that shows use and wear.

In 1947, Lord Mackintosh of Halifax commissioned the well-known British potter, Leonard Jarvis, to design and create a Toby jug depicting Winston Churchill. Lord Mackintosh was not only a personal friend and ally of Churchill, but also a leading Toby jug collector. Jarvis created a fine porcelain Toby jug of 18th century style, in a limited edition of 350. Churchill is depicted primarily as a painter; however, the book, quill and ink pot at his feet also pay homage to his being a writer and the trowel denotes his brick laying hobby. Lord Mackintosh gave the first ten Toby jugs to Churchill, kept one for himself and gave the rest away as Christmas presents. Known as the "Jarvis Jug," this Churchill Toby is one of the rarest and most sought-after pieces of all Churchill collectibles.

*Greetings for Christmas
and a happy New Year for
the English-speaking peoples*

CASSELL & COMPANY LTD
37/38 St. Andrew's Hill, London, E.C.4

Churchill is depicted as a Viking on the front of this 1956 Christmas card from Cassell & Company, Ltd., the publisher of his four volume series, *History of the English Speaking Peoples*. Churchill began writing the series in 1937 and finally completed and published the multi volumes from 1956-58. The series focuses on the history of Britain and its former colonies and possessions, from Caesar's invasion of Britain (55 BC) to the end of the Boer War (1902).

These two posters and calling card were used in Britain's 1959 general election, when Churchill stood as MP for Woodford for the last time. He won re-election by almost 15,000 votes and served until October, 1964. He was almost 90 years old and age and illness limited his appearances in the House of Commons.

One of my supporters called on you to-day but found that you were not at home.

In case he is not able to call again, may I present my compliments and ask for your support at the poll on Thursday, 8th. October.

Winston S. Churchill

Published by Col. W. H. Barlow-Wheeler, 69 Cleveland Road, South Woodford, E.18.
Printed by Tulip Press Ltd. (T.U.) Newbold Works, Princes Road, Buckhurst Hill, Essex.

The Master of the Household has received Her Majesty's commands to invite

<u>Major Geoffrey Eastwood</u>

to a Buffet Luncheon to be given by The Queen and The Duke of Edinburgh at Buckingham Palace on Saturday, the 30th January, 1965 after the State Funeral of the Right Hon. Sir Winston Churchill

12.30 p.m. o'clock

Thank you, Sir Winston, for all you have given the world.